THE WORKaholic SYNDROME

Also by Judith K. Sprankle

WORKING IT OUT: The Domestic Double Standard

THE WORKAHOLIC SYNDROME

Judith K. Sprankle
and
Henry Ebel

Walker and Company
New York

To
ADAM, JENNA and RICK
with love

First published in the United States of America in 1987 by the Walker Publishing Company, Inc.

Published simultaneously in Canada by John Wiley & Sons Canada, Limited, Rexdale, Ontario.

Library of Congress Cataloging-in-Publication Data

Sprankle, Judith K., 1946–
The workaholic syndrome.

1. Workaholics—United States. 2. Work ethic—United States.
I. Ebel, Henry, 1938– . II. Title.
HF5548.8.S628 1987 155.2′32 86-19069
ISBN 0-8027-0917-6

Printed in the United States of America

10 9 8 7 6 5 4 3 2 1

Book design by Deborah England

PREFACE

Today, as never before, work has become the focus of life for a vast number of adults. Twenty or so years ago, the "workaholic" was the exception. Most Americans took jobs to provide for their families, who remained the center of their lives. But in 1986 we are frighteningly close to inverting that order of priorities.

The going assumption for both men and women is that one's job—the kind of work one does and the status associated with it—provides the central definition of one's identity. Worse yet, while few people overtly underrate the values of home and family, in a *de facto* way these have often become secondary.

Though it is not yet widely acknowledged, this new American work ethic gathered astounding momentum during the late 1970s. As a result, we are struggling as a society and as individuals to accommodate the high priority now given to career issues by spouses, other family members, friends, colleagues . . . and ourselves. By their sheer numbers and the consequently narrowing opportunities at every upward rung of the organizational ladder, the Baby Boomers have been compelled to do more, to move faster, to compete harder. They, in turn, have set the pace for other age groups. The signs of increased stress are legion and have been intensified by an economic climate that mandates that if we marry at all, we marry a working spouse. The emotional and demographic repercussions have been dramatic.

While the concept of a nation of voluntary workaholics might have been absurd two decades ago, in the 1970s emotional stimuli (the women's liberation movement) and economic factors (inflation) prompted more people than ever before to seek self-fulfillment almost exclusively within the workplace. To an extraordinary extent, "what you do" has become "who you are," with an undeniable ripple effect on the rest of our lives. Clearly, the time has come to put work in its place.

Within these pages, we address this redefinition of the relationship between work and life: how it occurred, why it snowballed in so many people's lives, and why we are beginning to see a backlash as more and more Americans wake up to the negative effects of the trend. Instead of being preached at by experts or bombarded with statistics that have little meaning for the individual, you are invited to consider with us the ramifications of the new work ethic, along with some options for dealing successfully with it—or for refusing to adopt it at all.

Our objective is to provide an emotional, intellectual, and psychological perspective on today's work-obsessed culture, one that will help people at all stages of life to plan for a more balanced future.

Contents

Part One

Part Two

Part One

O brave new world,
That has such people in't!
—William Shakespeare

I don't like work—no man does—but I like what is in work—the chance to find yourself. Your own reality—for yourself, not for others.

—Joseph Conrad

The New American Work Ethic

As recently as thirty years ago, "work" was something of a dirty word, as in "*My* wife will never have to go out and work, thank God!" Even twenty years ago, the term *workaholic* was used to describe a weirdo—usually male—who *voluntarily,* for crying out loud, kept his nose to the grindstone when his colleagues were well into their second martinis. All in all, it was abundantly clear to most folks that one worked because one had to—to put food on the table and a roof over the heads of one's dependents—and worked only as long as was absolutely necessary to achieve those objectives. The family was the indisputable core of life, and work was something undertaken by most people to bring home the bacon, buy the wife a mink, and get the kids' teeth straightened.

In the 1940s, through their participation in the war effort, women discovered the enormous personal, as well as financial, satisfaction to be derived from work outside the home. As a result, the concept of work lost much of its burdensome moral tone. According to author Paul Bernstein, "it was no longer a calling sanctified by God, but appeared to be an earthly venture in pursuit of bread and bangles."

The 1950s saw a specific search for a new lifestyle centered on Family. Young married couples joined an enormous social and geographical movement as they moved out of the city and away from the old neighborhood to take up residence in the suburban rings surrounding the nation's major metropolitan centers. And they typically left behind in the city the network of relatives and friends who were entitled to drop into one's apartment or attached home without notice, as well as the availability of bars and saloons where husbands could easily gather in an all-male environment to share complaints about their wives.

In the new commuter suburbs, primary values were pegged to the needs of what eventually came to be called the nuclear, as opposed to the extended, family. The whole point of life now was to draw *toward* rather than *away from* the spouse one had married and the children one had subsequently produced. Family became a powerful value rather than an unquestioned necessity. Given the rise of American prosperity, as the country's booming economy dominated the world in general and the shattered European and Japanese economies in particular, a new life pattern quickly asserted itself and came to seem entirely normal. It featured a commuter husband whose daily journey into the city was often compared, only half in jest, to the heroism of the hunter who sallies forth into a threatening wilderness in order to obtain life's necessities for his dependents. At home, in the one-family cave, remained the newly enlightened housewife whose role it was to embody and preserve the values of Family, including the socialization of the boys and girls who would make up the next generation of breadwinners and homemakers.

Beginning in 1960, and with its roots in the World War II era, work evolved—not insidiously, not stealthily, but openly and with our enthusiastic, wholehearted support—into the central defining element of our identities. In ever-growing numbers, housewives abandoned their kitchens to discover that not only was working in law, finance, or marketing a whole lot more interesting than cooking and cleaning, but employers were actually willing to *pay* them to do these things. (At home, they were rarely even thanked for their services.) The flower children who had so fervently decried materialism in the 1960s just as fervently embraced it as they entered their thirties and found that love didn't—and Daddy wouldn't any longer—pay the rent.

Too, the *recognition* afforded in the workplace was at least as beguiling as the compensation. People who went out to work were perceived as "doing something" with their lives. They were in the mainstream, involved, with it, while those who remained voluntarily unemployed became the objects of thinly veiled scorn. At home, you could easily wear the same jeans and sweatshirt three days running without anyone noticing. At work, people noticed everything—what you wore, how you did your hair, a new scent or attaché case. At home, your opinions and thoughts fell on the often deaf ears of your loved ones. At work, people listened, reacted, agreed, or disagreed with gusto. When you did something well on the job, it seemed as if the whole world knew it. The fact that they also knew when you did something poorly and got chewed out by your superiors only added spice to the adventure.

Work was challenging; it was often downright difficult, and on bad days the frustrations could seem endless, the lows bottomless. But on good days, when the adrenaline surged and the ideas clicked, there was no excitement to beat it.

Thus, in the work-obsessed culture of the 1980s, "what you do" has become "who you are" to a frightening extent, and the ramifications of the resulting lack of balance in our lives are only beginning to be acknowledged. While work is admittedly not the only way to achieve self-fulfillment, it remains the vehicle of choice for the vast majority of today's men and women. We have become a thoroughly job-involved population, according to researchers Thomas Lodahl and Mathilde Kejner, who define "job involvement" as the degree to which a person is identified psychologically with his or her work. Depending on how central the job is to a person's sense of identity, they say, today's worker decidedly tends to agree with statements such as "The major satisfaction in my life comes from my job," "The most important things that happen to me involve my job," and even "I live, eat, and breathe my job!"

For more than twenty years, then, workers who entered the labor force after 1960 have participated eagerly in the new American work ethic and have, as a result, come to demand more from their jobs on every level than is reasonable. In addition to expecting material rewards from employment, we seek self-definition—a reflection of who we are in our own and society's eyes—in the workplace, where the primary value is, after all, profit rather than pleasure.

The symptoms of our obsession are all around us. Flipping through the Yellow Pages of the telephone directory, one finds an assortment of services geared to the needs of today's fully employed adult: cleaning, cooking, shopping, laundry, catering, child care. There are even professional advocates who will write a letter of protest to the utility company that has snarled up your account or who will take to task the contractor who began but never got around to finishing your new patio.

All these services are available for a price, and we Americans are, apparently, more than willing to pay it in order to free ourselves from domestic hassles and remain focused on the main thing: *The Job*.

At the supermarket, fully prepared meals in easy-open cartons glisten within refrigerated bins. They need only be popped into the microwave for a few minutes to yield the appropriate nutritional allotment. For those without enough time even for the express checkout line, an assortment of fast-food emporia stand ready to dish up everything from soup to Sushi—to go.

Even a cursory review of the titles on the drugstore magazine rack confirms our preoccupation with work. One business publication after another competes for our attention, while those *not* exclusively devoted to career issues, from *Good Housekeeping* to *Playboy*, regularly feature articles on succeeding in the workplace, using office politics to one's advantage, and how to combine domestic responsibilities with career pursuits.

In the mid-1960s, only divorced women whose ex-husbands had skipped the state utilized the few day-care centers then available to working mothers, and then only if they could not find a more suitable child care alternative. Today, day care is a multibillion-dollar industry patronized by the parents of millions of preschool children—a growing number of them less than a year old—by choice rather than by necessity.

Matrimony used to be the implicit objective of dating-service patrons. Today, the young woman in the video dating-service ad confides, "I like my job. My career is important to me, but the men I used to meet always complained when I worked nights and weekends. Then I enrolled in Lifestyles International. Now I'm meeting lots of men who are just as busy as I am!" Presuming that two such workaholics would rarely have the opportunity or the inclination to get together, one wonders why they bother with a dating service at all.

Even when marriage is still the desired outcome of dating, finding an appropriate mate seems to be getting tougher and tougher. In years past a young woman generally felt that she couldn't admire a man whom she could beat at, say, arm wrestling. Now, she finds it impossible to consider a serious relationship with a man who earns less than she does.

The price we paid for this emphasis on careers, obviously, was the relentless erosion of personal priorities. Where home and family had once been the focus of life, the extraordinary demands of our new work-centered existence placed The Job squarely at center stage. Gradually, the lines between personal and professional lives became indistinct, then nonexistent.

Social occasions became mere facades for business negotiations. Friendly conversation metamorphosed into professional conferences. Because the bulk of human interaction centered around colleagues and superiors at varying levels within the employing organization, spontaneous bonhomie was replaced by a wary and calculating formation of alliances.

At first—caught up as we were in the novelty of career pursuits, charmed by new self-images as productive members of society, and reassured by the prospect of financial independence offered by our paychecks—none of this seemed to matter a great deal. It was simply a necessary part of the fascinating new game that was being played, and little by little America's conversion to a nation of voluntary workaholics was accomplished.

At the heart of this change are the Baby Boomers, and by examining what's really happening with them, we can begin to define the parameters of this social phenomenon.

Clustered within the ranks of middle management in the mid-1980s, the Boomers eye each other anxiously as they view the shrinking number of advancement opportunities available within any given organization. In an attempt to get an edge on the competition, they spend longer and longer hours on the job. The eight-hour day has steadily lengthened into the ten- or twelve-hour day, and working on weekends—at home or at the office—has come to be the norm for the fast tracker.

The pressures this lifestyle places on personal relationships of every sort are extraordinary, influencing everything from dating to marital agreements to parenthood to community development.

Many men and women now accept the idea that the necessary commitment to getting ahead in a career precludes their marrying and/or having a family. The result is a new class of single men and women within our society. In a 1985 magazine article, writer Hilary Cosell tells the distaff side of the story, typified by her own experience:

> For anyone of my generation deeply affected by the Women's Movement, success would make you active, not passive. You would be in control of your fate and your future, the way men are. After studying history and political science for two years at Sarah Lawrence College, I transferred to New York University to study journalism. I next got a master's degree in it. Then I went out after my vision of success. I began as a production associate for a network news show; almost a year later, I got my big break. At twenty-four, I had a new title: Network Television Producer, and my life changed almost overnight. I traveled every week and talked to famous people and probably walked around looking smug. I had done everything right. I had money and power and independence and a profession. So imagine my shock, my near trauma, when I realized that I wanted something else—that somehow, after years of education and indoctrination

> into the virtues of success, I had started to feel empty and isolated and desolate, to feel a need for some kind of personal life that was more than casual or occasional, unstable and rootless.
>
> There I was, coming home from ten or twelve or sometimes more hours at work, pretty much shot after the day, doing this simply marvelous imitation of all the successful fathers I remembered from childhood—all the men I swore I'd never grow up and marry, let alone be like. There I'd be, swilling a vodka on the rocks or two, shoving a Stouffer's into my mouth, and then staggering off to take a bath, watch *Hill Street Blues,* and fade away with Ted Koppel. Somehow, the life I'd managed to construct for myself . . . seemed pretty much to preclude the possibility of living very differently. "I'll think about my personal life later," I'd tell myself.

Single men, too, often threw themselves into their work with total abandon, pushing aside the family ties that might fetter them professionally. Now, ten or fifteen years of relentless careerism is causing many to doubt the wisdom of their earlier choices. "What if I'm forty years old and still coming home to a one-bedroom apartment?" wonders Ted, a pediatrician.

> What if I wind up single, lonely, and unhappy, not sharing the things I've worked so hard to earn with anyone then, either? Being a pediatrician doesn't seem like the noble calling it once did—not if it means I never have children of my own because I was so damn preoccupied with taking care of other people's kids.

With the new attitude toward work came a growing ego-involvement with money, presaged on college and university campuses. Daniel Yankelovich's survey, "The

Changing Values on Campus," conducted in the early 1970s, was an early indicator that students' disdain for material concerns had largely evaporated. "The most widely held reason for going to college is to advance practical and career goals—money, work, success, position in the society," he wrote. After a decade of severe inflation, students' attitudes became even more pragmatic, attributable in no small measure to the alarming rise in the cost of attending college. With parents—and the students themselves—straining to put together the required tuition each year, and with loans piling up into five figures, the need to enter a lucrative career to recoup these losses took precedence over the 1960s' search for life's true meaning.

Jason, who attended a private New England university in the late 1970s, compares his collegiate experience with that of his older siblings:

> I'm the youngest of three in our family. My sister Amy is nearly ten years older than I, and our brother Matt just two years my senior. Dad is a corporate attorney, and compared to a lot of other families in our neighborhood, we were financially very comfortable, even though Mom didn't work outside the house. When Amy entered Smith in 1968, she was absolutely free to concentrate on her studies—no part-time job, even. And she spent all her free time involved in one cause after another, a real social organizer. Because it was never a problem, she never gave money a thought, except maybe to feel a little embarrassed that we had more than enough of it. She got a B.A. in English Literature, then a Master of Arts, with no particular career in mind. Eventually, she went to work for a small publishing house in Boston, mainly for the fun of it, and Dad continued to send her an allowance for years.

By the time Matt was ready for college, though, things were very different. By 1976, the year he entered Harvard, his annual tuition was probably twice what Amy's had been, and Dad's salary had pretty well peaked. Dad was still subsidizing Amy to some extent, and I was just two years away from college. Mom still didn't work, and the cost of everything was skyrocketing. Within a matter of months, a very heavy change in Dad's attitude became apparent. Instead of "Enjoy yourselves, kids!" it was "It's time to grow up and put your shoulder to the wheel," and while we were all shocked at the time, in retrospect I can't blame him. While Amy had been free as a bird during her school years, Matt was told to get a part-time job and to plan on working summers. Not only did Amy's allowance get cut off, but she was expected to start saving money against the day I entered college, just in case it was needed.

Matt transferred from Harvard to Northeastern in his sophomore year to take advantage of their work/study program. Instead of going to college to get an education, he was going to college to get a good job. It all got pretty grim real fast, and our priorities changed dramatically.

Two years later, with tuition still going up something like 10 percent a year, it was my turn, and an Ivy League school was out of the question. I opted for the civil engineering program at a local university, but because it was a private institution, the tuition was still very steep. Mom even considered going to work at the university, because tuition was reduced for the children of employees, but, instead, I lived at home for the first two years, working part-time during the school year and full-time summers to save enough for a car. I had to take a year off between my junior and senior years to work and save even more. It took me more than six years to get through, and even so, we were lucky to make the tuition payments for me and Matt without taking out loans.

The changing priorities of Jason and his family were typical of that era and they were intensified by the fact that the inflationary 1970s wrought havoc with even relatively large salaries. If you analyze your present salary in terms of 1970 buying power, you will find that your current buying power has hardly gone up at all. According to Albert H. Cox, Jr., formerly a chief economist for Merrill Lynch Pierce Fenner & Smith, "People are working hard and earning less. So, if college students are preoccupied with getting good jobs and earning a lot of money, there are some good reasons to back them up."

Earning a lot of money has become, in fact, a top priority for Americans caught up in the new work ethic. And if the desire for more money is what is leading more and more of us into the workplace, we are also discovering, once we get there, that the amount of money we earn almost invariably determines our positions in the organizational hierarchy. In the workplace, the level of earnings has become the absolute indicator of career progress. The standard rule of thumb is that you are successful at what you do if you are earning $1,000 for every year of your age. "If somebody walks in at age forty-five and tells me he's earning $30,000, I start wondering what's wrong with this guy," says a Chicago headhunter, and most of his colleagues would agree. As recently as the 1960s, careers which helped to better society such as teaching, fundraising for nonprofit organizations, administration of cultural institutions, or social service work, might logically be chosen by talented workers despite low salaries because they offered more intellectually stimulating or intrinsically rewarding life-styles. Today, the person who opts for such a career is often regarded as having a screw loose.

Advancement through the ranks has always had social consequences. As workers move upward, they invariably find themselves leaving former colleagues behind, emotionally and physically. As painful as this may be, it has always been accepted as the price of success. Vice presidents don't socialize with truck drivers, and clerks don't join managers for lunch. Today, however, in our pervasively work-centered society, those consequences reach farther and dig deeper than would have seemed possible as recently as 1970.

As we have already mentioned, modern young women candidly admit that they find it difficult to contemplate a serious relationship with a man who earns less than they do. They seek partners to whom they can look up—or who will at least be perceived as their equals, and money is the measuring stick. At the same time—the Census Report of 1981 documented that wives were earning more than their husbands in 16 percent of all two-career couples—4.1 million marriages, to be precise. The struggle to deal with this new reality has thrown thousands of couples into cultural shock.

Even when he still earns more than she, money can significantly interfere with the marital relationship. In the 1970s and 1980s, we have seen the reemergence of prenuptial agreements, which basically state that what's hers is hers, what's his is his, and it will stay that way whether or not the marriage endures. Thus, marriage and other long-term relationships between the sexes have become overtly economic as well as emotional arrangements, much as they were centuries ago when the bride's dowry was considerably more important than her affections. The difference is that today both partners are expected to bring comparable net worth and earning potential to the bargaining table.

As potentially divisive as money can be in a relationship, it can also be the tie that binds in today's two-income marriages. "The good life in America increasingly requires a household economic team of two workers," economist George Sternlieb and James W. Hughes explained in a recent magazine article, and most of us would have to agree that the real key to material progress is having two earners in the family. It is this, rather than any generalized rise in income, that helps overcome the lingering effects of long-term inflation. With one earner in a family, $40,000 is an impressive income, but it will not cover much more than basic living expenses. With two earners, $80,000 in income is not beyond the range of possibility. Two incomes offer the chance to take an occasional vacation, dine out once in a while, live a little.

Over and above the ego needs of the individuals involved, therefore, modern marital relationships have restructured themselves around economic realities. For many couples—and most emphatically for those with children—divorce has become economically unfeasible. Either partner, or both, may be involved in an extramarital affair. Either may be slack in the area of domestic responsibilities. He may be a rotten father and she may be a slovenly housekeeper, but as long as they both bring home that essential paycheck, it will take something far more earth-shattering to dissolve an arrangement based less on transitory feelings than on rock-ribbed finances.

Claude and Ellen offer a case in point. Both bashful and introverted by nature, the two met and married during 1967, their last year at Boston University, in the flush of first love. Because both had been single children and longed for a large family, Ellen was delighted, on graduation day, to discover that she was pregnant and immediately postponed all thoughts of a career.

> Claude was the first man with whom I had ever had a romantic involvement, and I was leery of rushing into marriage—but not leery enough. And we had such similar backgrounds and interests, I really think we might have made a go of it if we'd given ourselves a few years to work and save some money and get to know each other outside of the college setting. On campus, everything had been taken care of for us, but once we graduated and Claude became an actuarial trainee at John Hancock in Boston, things were very different. He was all caught up in his work and studies, but after I got the apartment painted and decorated as well as we could afford on his salary, I had nothing to do but wait for the baby to be born. I'd pounce on him the minute he came in the door at night, hungry for his conversation and company, and all he'd want to do would be to bolt dinner and hit the books again.

When their daughter Jenny was born at Christmas, Ellen had no time to worry about their deteriorating relationship, she recalls. Had she looked closely at the situation then, she says, she would have realized how far she and Claude had already grown apart.

> Every day, I stayed home with Jenny, and every day Claude went off to the office, where he enjoyed the company of dozens of attractive, intelligent women who shared his professional interests. Since I literally had been Claude's first and last girlfriend up to that time, it wasn't surprising that his head was turned. I realize now that once Jenny was a year or so old, I should

> have gone to work myself, made some effort to be a part of his world and to share the economic responsibilities of marriage. But instead, I got pregnant again. Erin was born in the spring of 1969.

With two demanding infants sharing their now inadequate living quarters, Ellen says, the din was often unbearable, and Claude came home later and later each evening. Finally, he stopped coming home at all, and Ellen learned that he was having an affair with a secretary in his office. Angry and resentful, she confronted her husband and demanded a divorce, but the fact was, though both were willing to dissolve their marriage, they simply could not afford to do so.

> By that time, we had been married less than four years. While Claude's salary would have been marginally adequate to support the two of us—and very adequate if we had had no children and I had been earning a salary, too—there was no way he could support all four of us if we had separate residences. Even living under the same small roof was a big stretch in a city as expensive as Boston, but we could just barely manage to survive with two kids if we stayed together. So ours became a marriage in name only. Claude came and went, and I stayed on as full-time housekeeper and nanny, though I vowed that the minute both girls were in school I would get a job and leave.

When Jenny and Erin finally did enter school full-time in 1977, Ellen set out to fulfill her promise to herself, but she came up against the hard reality of inflation. The cost of living was sky-high, especially the cost of after-school day care in the city. Worse, never having worked before, she was forced to accept an entry-level position as an insurance underwriter, and her salary was tiny compared to Claude's. Even with child support from him, she could not stretch her earnings to cover a separate apartment for herself and the children. Once again, divorce was economically impossible.

> By 1980, I was earning a pretty good salary, but the insurance industry went into a gigantic slump, and I was laid off. By then we had moved to a decent-sized apartment with three bedrooms, but the rent was fantastic in the city, and we needed to live close enough in to use public transportation. Jenny, at age eleven, was in braces, and the orthodontist said Erin would need them as well. In just seven years, Jenny would be ready for college, with her sister right behind her. Though I eventually found another job, I had to take a big cut in pay, and we were right back where we had been when we first talked about separating. No way.

Today, Ellen tries to be philosophic about her admittedly unusual relationship with Claude, referring to their marriage as a purely financial arrangement. "I work, he works, and we share the bills. That's it," she says, shrugging.

> Next year, Jenny enters BU, and the year after that, Erin. I'm forty-one years old now—by the time they both graduate, I'll be forty-six, and my personal life will have been on hold for more than twenty years. I'm just not comfortable with casual affairs, though I have met two men over the years to whom I was strongly attracted. Claude has gone from one woman to the other—I lost count years ago. But I have to give the devil his due. He's never seriously neglected the girls, and he's always carried his share of the expenses.

> It's really bizarre. We don't even actively dislike each other after all this time! And when we're both out from under the incredible financial burden of raising two kids and can finally afford to get divorced, we probably won't bother. We'll have to get going on a retirement program! She laughs bitterly as she makes that final statement.

Clearly, work—and the money we earn by performing it—has taken over our lives in ways that would have been unimaginable only decades ago. Emotionally and economically, we are tethered to our jobs as we could not possibly have foreseen when we embraced the new American work ethic in the 1970s. Even so, the magnitude of the trend is only beginning to be acknowledged as, after ten to twenty years of espousing the "work is everything" philosophy, we begin to feel the strain of our hectic lives—and to acknowledge the gaps in them, as well.

The first signs of backlash are beginning to appear as corporate executives firmly decline transfers, even when they are tied to attractive salary increases, as more women opt to remain at home with their young children, even when their prospects for job advancement suffer as a result, and as partners in commuter marriages refuse to continue to live apart, even though one may suffer a career setback because of that decision. As always, the signs of discontent are cropping up at the grass-roots level long before governmental and commercial institutions are inclined to put into place the new policies and structures that might head off the trouble looming large on our societal horizon. And that, of course, is what's necessary if Americans are to cope successfully with the extraordinary demands we are placing on ourselves.

Whether we survive in a humane fashion as individuals, families, and communities depends heavily on how we—individually and collectively—exercise our options in the months and years ahead. Somehow, we must regain control of our lives by reexamining our priorities and making new choices. As author Alison Lurie puts it, "As long as America is full of Yuppies of all ages and both sexes who are willing to work a sixty-hour week, replace social with business entertaining, and leave their one or two children to be brought up by hired help, why would any employer in his right mind bother to restructure?" Why, indeed?

Once again, as a society and as individuals, we are teetering on the brink of change in our attitudes toward work and money. If balance is to be regained in our lives, it is up to each of us to say, "Whoa, there! This isn't working for me and my family any more." But before we can make good decisions about where we are going from here, it's important that we understand fully the ways—only touched on here—in which work is consuming us. Only then can we hope to begin putting work in its place, wherever that place rightfully is in our lives, and to disentangle ourselves from the workaholic syndrome.

Part Two

Things fall apart; the center cannot hold;
Mere anarchy is loosed upon the world,
The blood-dimmed tide is loosed, and everywhere
The ceremony of innocence is drowned. . . .

—*William Butler Yeats*

I claim not to have controlled events, but confess plainly that events have controlled me.

—Abraham Lincoln

Losing Control

Americans live in a vast country with an enormous number of fellow citizens. As they struggle to cope with the sheer magnitude of their society, the people of this country often come to feel that things are getting out of control. And when that feeling involves work, family life, and personal behavior, the reaction—at least verbally—can be near hysteria.

The American fear of loss of control relates to the common American assumption that things *ought* to be under control. We read magazines like *Money* that tell us how to go about our financial planning. We buy life insurance and disability coverage, as well as mortgage insurance and elaborate pension plans, because we want to minimize the risks with which life and the passage of the years confront us.

At the same time, there is a contradictory strand in the American fiber—a set of values that can be summed up as those of the frontier. Included in the perpetual list of American folk heroes are the entrepreneurs, explorers, developers, and psychological astronauts who leave security behind in order to take some enormous risk.

Those who fail never make the headlines, but those who succeed are quite likely to stare out at us from the cover of *Time* or *Newsweek*—or *Money*.

In our struggle to find a personal path between the poles of security and abandon, control and release, we have tended to assign a special value to Family. Precisely because each of us must be so concerned with ourselves in our search for self-fulfillment, we have had to maintain the idea of Family as an almost conscious—and sometimes artificial—way of striking a balance and keeping ourselves sane.

The typically American tension between the values of control and entrepreneurship was played out in the new work patterns that developed after World War II. The husband foraging forth into the world of business could be seen as a continuation of the patterns originated by Daniel Boone and other frontiersmen. The wife staying home to look after the family nest and the children contained inside it represented the opposite strain of mythology: a world free of danger or competition in which life could be devoted to getting things fully organized.

But there was a context that contained both sides of this dialectic inside a yet larger framework. True, the husband "fighting traffic" on his way to "fighting the competition" could be seen as a macho figure glamorously embarked on destruction. But his efforts were being made at a time when America's largest corporations dominated the postwar world. America's antitrust legislation was balanced by America's actual world position. Ostensibly ferocious competition took place within the framework of vastly expanding business opportunities that were based, in turn, on America's global hegemony.

How much of this system was agreed-upon myth became clear when all of its parts began to crumble simultaneously. Those who took part in the 1960s' rebellion devoted much of their energy to destroying the postwar idealization of suburban life. If it had produced Vietnam, they reasoned, then it must have been, all along, secretly corrupt. No sooner had the young radicals of the late 1960s and early 1970s done their work, than the successive financial crises of the 1970s revealed the extent to which America was no longer in charge of its own destiny—but tied to the other nations of the world in an interdependent system that could, on occasion, send it reeling.

Overall global control was gone forever—a lesson that would echo down through the 1980s as faceless terrorists sent American tourists scuttling for cover or convinced them to settle for Disneyworld. Meanwhile, women showed decreasing enthusiasm for a role that kept them tied to house and home. Even those who didn't get divorced and didn't stay single insisted on having careers and having fewer children or none at all. American men, meanwhile, also began to question the previously unquestioned significance of Family—with its attendant mythology of self-sacrifice.

All of these trends converged on a new American romance with the idea of the marketplace, in which canny individuals deploy their full attention in the struggle to match supply to demand. The "outs" of a previous student generation—the business majors who were hopeless at understanding Shakespeare and Freud—became the "ins" of the 1980s, hell-bent on getting *their* share of Yuppie pleasures and perks.

Between 1975 and 1985, assisted by the presidency of Ronald Reagan, the values of the marketplace seeped steadily downward into the psyches of the American population. And what the marketplace connoted was, above all, competition—the quest of a large number of people after a limited amount of money that could only be parted with voluntarily by those who had it to give. Now, men and women together struggled inside a system of ultimate control—that of the marketplace—which rewarded those who could be strongest and shrewdest in the struggle with everybody else. In turn, the fierce strife of Americans with each other—of individuals for advancement within their companies, of companies for advancement against each other—laid the basis for the struggle of America as a whole against the other national economies located on Planet Earth.

Suddenly it became clear to a great many people simultaneously that the *real* world was exciting rather than secure, unpredictable rather than assured, and a place made for the young "heroic single" rather than the middle-aged "married man" or "married woman" of the 1950s. Wringing a profit out of it for one's company, as well as a good living for oneself, was the challenge that confronted a working man or woman every morning of every day until retirement.

In this new context, the fact that the international marketplace provided an *ultimate* framework of control was an abstract consolation. In reality, the myth of the entrepreneur—the hunter, fighter, warrior, competitor—was back.

What the world of business did offer, it soon became clear to almost everyone, were the challenges—the terrors, but also the joys—of combat, including the supreme joy of being a winner rather than a loser. The new folk heroes were people like Lee Iacocca and fictional characters like Sylvester Stallone's Rocky, who simply wouldn't let competition keep them down.

Competition, of course, easily escalates to hostility, and the evidence of a *socially sanctioned hostility* is all around us. Court calendars are crammed with litigation against physicians, lawyers, companies, governments, and spouses. Derogatory advertising that directly names one's competitors (a no-no two decades ago) is now an accepted marketing ploy. In divorce proceedings, quarrels over child custody have given way, in an age of fewer and fewer children, to harsh contests over pension plans and the shared value of a spouse's professional degree. Since the 1970s began, winning has been back as a primary American value.

But life in the business world, like life anywhere else, is not a vacation or an interlude. Its defining characteristic is that it goes on and on and on . . . and on and on. And while life as a hunter in a Stone Age or Bronze Age setting was marked by prolonged periods of rest and relaxation—because most of the food was actually provided by the women who did the agricultural work and because a meat orgy in the age before refrigerators left you too full to do other than sleep—the proper analogy for life in the business world is, in fact, the kind of perpetual attentiveness that is most easily duplicated by a *machine*.

Though there is a good deal of self-fulfillment possible in the world of business, *the purpose of business has never been self-fulfillment*. Its purpose is sales—and even sales are only a vehicle to profits.

Dr. Hans Selye, who pioneered the concept of stress, made a distinction in his later years between bad stress (distress) and good stress (eustress). Good stress raises our adrenaline levels, stimulates our senses to keener functioning, sets our minds racing in search of insight, innovation, and the solutions to our current problems. It arouses the fight-or-flight reflex that served our prehistoric ancestors so well, even if the saber-toothed tiger we fight today is a rival company or if modern flight consists of selling out and cutting our losses. All the positives that involve us in the *eustressful* aspects of what we are doing—the thrill of the chase, the lust for victory—turn out to be so deeply involving that we cannot altogether avoid the obsessive *distressing* aspects that are the other side of the coin: fear of failure, fear of having already made a fatal error, and general diffuse anxiety.

In short, what those actually in the business world soon learn to live with is perpetual, boundless, bottomless *anxiety*. There is no one "on the outside" or "up above" who can truly tell you that you have ever done *enough*.

The pervasive excitement of living in such an unpredictable, alertness-demanding environment has yet another effect: the implication that *it* is real and that other things, including those traditionally associated with Home and Family, are *less* real. Many men and women have described the complex alternation between their domestic and work lives as a sense of living in two separate dimensions, like someone in a science fiction novel. Perhaps neurological research eventually will be able to show that left-hemispheric functions predominate in the daytime world of the office while the more intuitive and instantaneous right-hemispheric modes are galvanized in the home environment.

Whatever the physiological basis for the feeling that Work and Home are powerfully alternative to each other, the contrast that is so often felt between the two spheres raises the dangerous possibility that one of them can, in fact, overwhelm the other. The fact that Home is financially dependent on Work gives the latter a particularly important arrow in its quiver. The fact that you can bring Work into your Home in the form of anxiety, including the fearful anticipation of combats still before you, adds yet another. Swept up in the furor of daytime battles, it is much harder to recall, in a way that really matters, the experiences of love and support that make Home and Family, beyond their role as myths, so important to those—even those—who live in the Age of Divorce and whose remarriages testify to that importance.

But what can be deadly in personal relationships, where the partner desiring to "win" is often confronted by the sound of a slamming door as the other partner stomps off in search of better feelings, can seem to work well in the culture of the workplace. For the compulsive winner, work may be the only viable form of marriage in today's world.

For those caught up in a competitive marriage, the workplace may become particularly significant as a setting in which victories *are* possible; there, specific contracts can be won, specific budgetary or sales goals reached, specific rivals forced out. An unsatisfactory, envy-ridden marriage can be one more crucible for the forging of the workaholic personality.

Within marriage, the forces of envy increasingly cluster around issues of career and salary—especially as the honeymoon gives way to the long, hard slog in which a relationship has to be tended like a plant subject to a variety of ills. Salaries, titles, promotions, and working conditions are all possible areas for invidious comparison. Moreover, our new world of work, with its breakdown of what were once defined as the male and female spheres of life, makes the collision direct rather than oblique.

Envy and anger can generate an escalating spiral that is difficult to reverse, particularly when one partner suspects that the other has society on his or her side and is receiving general approval for a superior career or professional performance. The other partner may very well protest that he or she feels pressure rather than approval, and envy or hostility from peers and coworkers rather than any bath of good feeling. The point is, what matters is not the objective reality, which may be impossible to define, but the *perception*.

Another way of putting the same thing is to say that the perfectionists among us—those who can never do enough to satisfy themselves—are the ones most likely to interpret another person's real or imaginary gains as criticisms of their own performance. This is particularly true in today's world where the entrepreneur who hungers for increasing levels of challenge has resumed the position of American folk hero and where a major Japanese automobile manufacturer boasts in television commercials that "We are driven!"

There may be a good number of marriages, in other words, that feature two hard-striving participants, each of whom fears being the loser to the other's winner—and each of whom finds it harder and harder to take genuine pleasure in the other's career advances or job triumphs. In addition, of course, a work- and status-obsessed society inevitably breeds individuals who are threatened by acute feelings of shame—Willy Lomans unable to face achieving less than some imagined, possibly unrealistic, ideal. For those struggling against the onrush of shame, marriage or any other close relationship can be particularly tormenting. Physical intimacy or proximity always verges on disclosing the most closely kept secret in a society that has placed a taboo on failure without quite defining success.

A competitive marriage is one headed toward dissolution, because the most enduring basis for marriage is friendship, where the desire to win can be set aside or brought under sharp control. Otherwise, the white wedding is often the prelude to a marriage in which the unspoken questions resonate: "Are we winning as a couple or a family? And within our partnership, which one of us is winning over the other?"

In both work life and personal life, the first step toward regaining a livable perspective may lie in redefining the concept of control. A generation of Americans has now come of age—the Baby Boomers—whose outlook has been shaped by the dominant myth of the later 1970s and early 1980s: that smart people with career savvy can make their untroubled way from business school to retirement without such mundane experiences as pain and disappointment.

The myth has been fed by a host of books and magazine articles written by people whose forte it is to sound smart, and who, by selectively pointing to those who have "made it," manage to imply that "making it" is a matter of will and intelligence alone.

But the implication that success is within everyone's reach and that one's life can be under complete, conscious control has been an especially painful myth for those now facing unprecedented levels of competition in the quest for higher salaries, better jobs, and desirable promotions. The statistics are against them. So is the volatile international business climate that has seen, within a few years, the meteoric rise and equally spectacular decline of Silicon Valley—or to give only one other example, the construction by Union Carbide of a self-glorifying corporate headquarters only a short time before the company became a global synonym for poison.

A sane attitude for those working in today's economy is not, however, fatalism or even pessimism, but rather an outlook that might be described as reasonable dedication: a full commitment of energy that maintains the perspective necessary to keep track of the limits of what it can hope to accomplish. An attitude like that is entrepreneurial in the right direction. It may glory in achievement, but it also strives for balance and for that inner harmony that is so often essential for correct decision-making.

Control in today's workplace, in other words, is more like swimming in an occasionally turbulent river than like running in a marathon. In the marathon the earth obligingly sits still, and you only twist your ankle if you fail to put your foot down in the right way. But the river is full of the unexpected, and survival may depend on permitting it to play an active role by carrying you some distance downstream where the application of your own energies is less likely to result in drowning.

If unremitting workaholic intensity is not always a formula for career success, still less is it a way of coping with the sphere of personal relationships. For better or worse, we live in an age when people no longer stick together because that is considered the proper or decent thing to do. The obverse side of that particular coin is that serious relationships in our world are highly expressive and responsive. If the feelings are altogether wrong, there is no longer much consolation in the fact that he is a good provider or that her floors are clean enough to eat off.

The second step toward sanity, therefore, is to avoid bringing into emotional relationships the sense of contractual obligation that is typical of business life—or of the transactions between those who have already undergone divorce. Strong emotional ties that are lasting and constructive are initiated through generosity rather than miserliness; through the sense, which is sometimes quite irrational, that the other person is there when needed. What is so difficult, obviously, is to maintain that level of feeling in the long years following the honeymoon. The inevitable bouts of weariness make it tempting to substitute a business-based metaphor of contractual reciprocity for the original notion of free giving and joyful abundance.

That may give special point to the idea, developed by family therapists, of some kind of a periodic retreat in which couples consciously reassess their relationship and try to renew the feelings that originally brought them together. Such a practice may be especially important in an age when couples often consist of two career-minded individuals who keep track of their separate checking accounts, pension plans, and property holdings.

All of us have seen movies set in the era in which swordsmanship was one mark of a gentleman. A prominant cliché in such films is the fencing master who proclaims (usually with a thick French accent) something like "The sword is like a bird. Hold her too lightly and she flies away. Hold her too tightly and she dies." That fencing master is talking, of course, about the same idea we have been examining—control within the quest for success; and the fact that what he says is a cliché ought not to blind us to the fact that it is also true.

Life is beautiful and ideal, or the reverse, only when we have taken into our consideration the social as well as the family relationship.

—Havelock Ellis

THE DECENTRALIZED FAMILY

Overwhelming changes in social behavior and in our view of it have taken place in the second half of the twentieth century. As a central defining image of the family myth as propagated in the 1950s, a good choice might be that of the family dinner table, where each day, at the appointed hour, families went through a ritual in which roles were affirmed and hierarchies reestablished. Now, in place of that rigidly structured event—the food cooked by Mom, carved by Dad, and served to the household gathered around the table—we are likely to find, most nights, a cheerful (or not so cheerful) free-for-all in which people eat when (a) they come home and (b) they are hungry. Alternatively, the family may decide to zip out to a fast-food restaurant that leaves them with no mess at all to clean up—and thus no need to argue over whose turn it is to do the cleaning. Even when a semblance of the family dinner does survive, it is just as likely to be Dad who does the cooking as Mom.

In the growing number of households with no children at all, the dining-room table may have an unused look, or it may be covered with boxes of take-out food from a nearby Chinese restaurant.

What were once considered absolute standards of behavior have been loosened, providing options that were once not even considered as possibilities. Children of eight or nine show a degree of sophistication and awareness of the world that was unavailable even to teenagers in 1955. Today, husbands and wives grant each other liberties that inevitably would have led to separation and divorce in an earlier age.

We can group all of these developments under the headings of *decentralization, individuation,* and a harder-to-describe category that might be labeled *the demand for upscale relationships*. In turn, these changes in the pattern of relationships within our society have powerfully affected our attitudes toward work, and they, in turn, have been strongly affected by alterations in the workplace.

Decentralization

In retrospect, and despite America's global reputation as a bastion of individual freedom, what stands out about life in the later nineteenth and early twentieth centuries is the degree to which the lives of most people were, in many ways simultaneously, under control. As late as the 1930s, unions were struggling to free workers from the tyranny of the company, libertarians were fighting for an end to literary and artistic censorship, and women's advocates were conducting an uphill battle in the name of reproductive and sexual freedom. The opponents in each case argued that any reduction in centralized control would lead to anarchy and chaos and would eventually be regretted by the rebels themselves. As late as the Eisenhower years, and particularly after the rise of Senator Joseph McCarthy, young people would assure each other that it was safer not to stand out in any way and not to sign any political petition, however innocuous.

In this sense, the great change that has taken place in our broadest social assumptions has been the one that sees individuals as generally trustworthy and self-regulating. This newer vision of how people function in everyday life was pioneered by writers like the late Paul Goodman, with their sense of the primacy of the small-scale community in which people know each other face to face. It has received additional support in the Reagan years from those on the political right and left who see big government as inherently liable to abuse.

The new vision of decentralization is visible in the classroom, in the workplace, and in the lives that most of us lead at home. In schools it is common to see classrooms in which desks and chairs are placed at varying angles in relation to each other, not all facing the front of the room where the teacher is the sole focus of attention. In the workplace, quality-circles based on the Japanese model—small groups of workers who share responsibility for substantial segments of production—are becoming common in factory settings. Where executives are concerned, there is a growing emphasis on the self-starter who plays a major role in defining his or her own workload and who encourages subordinates to do the same. Where home life is concerned, today's communities, even in suburban areas, tolerate a variety of lifestyles that would have seemed threatening in the world of the 1950s, provided that a basic conformity to social norms is observed and the rights of neighbors respected.

In a steadily more decentralized world, people of all ages take it for granted that they have to devise their own agendas, supervise their own work, and actively seek out the feedback that tells them how they are doing. More and more, they choose their work contacts and their social contacts rather than having them dictated by custom or the need for outside approval. And more and more, they are encouraged to do this by those who have some power over them, including bosses, teachers, and parents.

Individuation

As the word *individuation* implies, we live in a world that puts a powerful emphasis on the value of individual effort, initiative, and expression. Our culture heroes include people like Lee Iacocca and Karen Silkwood, who steadily refused to take no—absolute, unqualified no—for an answer.

It is important to note that these culture heroes differ from the rebels of twenty years ago, who were dropouts from society or actively hostile to its operations. Instead, today's heroes are persons struggling to articulate constructive, positive, socially and economically valuable points of view, the resistance to which comes from powerful, entrenched interests that refuse to acknowledge the need for change. They are, in short, members of the breed of individuals known as *entrepreneurs*, even when they are engaged, like Silkwood, in campaigning against abuses.

The value of the entrepreneurial, self-regulating, self-starting personality has begun to be recognized even by Fortune 500 corporations in their "*intra*preneurial" efforts aimed at generating new products and ways of accomplishing goals. Within families, the old hierarchical structure—Papa the breadwinner, Mama the homemaker, and Children their responsibilities—has given way to a laissez-faire approach that aims to give all parties the freedom they need to realize personal, individual aims.

The Demand for Upscale Relationships

As families, businesses, and individuals put a growing emphasis on the values of decentralization and individuation, they are obviously receiving some kind of confirmatory feedback that convinces them that this is a course worth following. Otherwise, the trend would grind to a halt, and we would find a movement in the opposite direction. The feedback being received must be positive and must carry with it the sense that what is going on furthers the value of pleasure, the value of success, and perhaps both of these values simultaneously.

Where children are concerned, the positive results of decentralization and individuation are visible all around us. Kids, we are often told, have become less kidlike, and childhood itself is in danger. At the same time, conversations with parents reveal the other side of the coin. Once seen as inherently irresponsible, thoughtless, or even dangerous (viz., Dennis the Menace), children have suddenly become good company—even fun to converse with. Their sharpened awareness of the world around them has made the kid/adult barrier far more porous than it used to be. It has also dissolved the adult fantasy that children don't really understand what is going on in the world of their elders.

In effect, the relationships that adults have with children have moved in an *upscale* direction. In terms of both the quality and quantity of interaction, these relationships provide a higher degree of satisfaction to the participants than was usually the case one or two generations ago.

What has been happening in the relationships between children and their parents helps to illuminate the broader changes that have been taking place in the relationships that adults have with each other and with their work situations. At each level it is possible to see a disintegrative element that often gives rise to feelings of alarm, but in each case, the disintegration has to be seen as relative to an earlier mode of behavior that holds little appeal to any of us. Here is a narrative by a middle-aged woman who edits a number of respected trade publications and who has experienced with special intensity the transition we are describing:

> Maybe I differ from other women of my generation, because even when I was in college in the 1950s, the assumption was that I would have my own career and that it would be at least as important to me as my domestic existence. Still, I look back to that time and to the years of my first marriage as a different universe. All relationships, in and out of work, were defined, I now feel, by things *not* said and subjects *not* broached. The various liberation movements I became involved in later on got some of their exaggerated qualities from that earlier stage. Now it became fashionable to blab endlessly about what you were doing and why you were doing it, so that self-revelation became the new way of being a bore.
>
> I see those two stages as transitional to where we are today—where *I* am, at any rate, and a lot of the people I regard as my peers. Where my work relationships are concerned, I don't feel there is a whole lot of blockage because of rules about what you can say and not say, be and not be. Work goes better because the people I cooperate with are grown-ups who don't have to be either sexual or antisexual with each other. We work because earning our livings is what we have to do and because we're professionals who enjoy working well.
>
> In the area of personal life, I see a lot more

> choice as now being the norm, as well as a lot more calmness in relationships. I don't hang around with people who bore or disturb me. Nor, on the other hand, do I feel a need to become physically intimate with someone just because we're getting along reasonably well. It's like the theory of psychoanalysis—that the whole point is to make the unconscious conscious, because that means you're choosing what you do rather than being driven to do it. I see myself and those around me as less driven, compelled, and compulsed.

Disintegration, better designated as decentralization, can be seen as the basis for a newer style of relating that is more difficult, in the sense of requiring more conscious, voluntary effort, but also more satisfying. This is not to say that what we are witnessing is a uniform system. On the contrary: the internal contradictions and tensions it generates are in many ways the subject of this book.

The tensions between an older and a newer mode of relating are sharply visible on the job as workers are required to do more and more in the way of self-regulation. When blue-collar employees were designated as "hands" and regulated by the speed of the assembly line, they gave birth to a whole social movement generally colored by Marxist theorizing that saw industrial capitalism as a dehumanizing and alienating system. In return for his or her weekly wages, the worker was forced to conform to the tyranny of the time clock and the compulsion of the conveyor belt. He or she had traded off the expressive and creative aspects of humanity for a boon—the pay packet or check—that was itself at the mercy of the economic and industrial cycle, with its periodic recessions and depressions.

What that system implied, of course, was that all of

the really important decisions were made in the board room and that the employees, including most white-collar workers, were there to carry them out. In contrast, today's business world is increasingly obsessed with the problem of *productivity* and increasingly aware that the problem can only be solved from the grass-roots level up.

Productivity, in both factory and office settings, is based on motivation and, in a highly competitive international economy, is related to quality as well as to quantity. Companies of all sizes, therefore, are laboring to put their fingers on the motivational triggers that will enable them to get the most out of their employees and to turn out products or services as close as possible to a Japanese or German standard. The great symptom of this change in attitude is the transformation of the Personnel Department, with its routine approach to hiring and firing, into something like the Department of Human Resources Development, with the implication that its core concern is getting the most out of those *presently* on the payroll.

Though some of what is going on in companies can be dismissed as external hype, there does seem to be a real change taking place. The new tone is exemplified by an executive who recently observed:

> One of the lines I keep hearing is "We don't need another 'employee.' " Everybody seems or claims to be on the lookout for workers who can accept a regular paycheck without assuming it only requires regular hours and average efforts. I also hear more and more about profit-sharing as an alternative to the automatic end-of-the-year bonus. "Incentive" is an in-word. The ideal seems to be a payroll loaded with entrepreneurs and soaked through with the breakthrough mentality. Shouts of "Eureka!" are supposed to ring

out at odd hours throughout the day and into the late evening.

The irony here suggests the tension that this new attitude brings with it. For the worker seeking to balance out work life and personal life, it poses special challenges. What today's companies are increasingly looking for, after all, is *a new kind of workaholic*. If the older-style workaholic could be defined as an obsessive-compulsive whose fussiness or retentiveness often impeded the very goals he or she claimed to be pursuing, the newer model—the intrapreneur—is one that is valued, above all, for creativity and the ability to think unprecedented thoughts. In turn, this tends to turn the company metaphor from one of channeling and containment—the predictable career ladder—into one of lateral and practically unlimited opportunity.

Today's employees, therefore, may receive strong positive feedback for generating new ideas, projects, and proposals that move to their superiors for approval. They may then be put in charge of the task of bringing those ideas closer to fruition. Under a profit-sharing system, they may also participate directly in reaping the financial rewards if the ideas succeed.

In the companies that have moved furthest toward putting such a system into operation, the potential for complete absorption by the employee is enormous. "After all," one employee in a real estate development firm said, "every one of us wants to demonstrate, above all, that we are effective. Getting something started from scratch and building it up to the point at which everybody salutes it is practically the definition of effectiveness."

More and more, therefore, the typical worker is not the slave of a tyrannical boss nor the terrified serf who fears a pink slip in his pay envelope but an individual who is faced with the need to do a significant amount of self-regulation. The risk is that he or she will become so absorbed in work life, so willing to say yes to an overload of projects, that personal life, family life, and relationships in general will suffer.

When personal and work lives are being reconfigured to the extent that is true of the present day, and when the *high-demand personality* is becoming a social norm, the struggle that many people live out in their daily lives has to do with reconciliation. Spouses, for example, may have to make a conscious effort *not* to apply to their relationship the standards that obtain within their work situations. The demands for sharp, clear reciprocity and feedback that make sense in a quantitative, profit-making situation spell potential doom for a relationship based on a multitude of variables and intangibles.

In a world of prenuptial contracts and frequent divorce, this distinction may be harder to make and maintain than at any time since love, rather than economics, became the basis of most marriages. What may be difficult to hold onto is the awareness that in the work world, support situations are the basis for pursuing ultimately financial goals, while in a marriage money is used to establish and maintain a support situation. Marriage is its own goal, not an instrument toward some other.

That distinction is especially hard to maintain at a time when couples are commonly defined as "a two-earner family" and talked about as a financial partnership, the purposes of which include the leverage needed for major purchases, large-scale investments, and a lucrative retirement. While financial considerations cannot be eliminated from the discussion of a successful marriage, the breakup of many marriages with an impeccable financial base shows that good financing is not enough if affection and mutual respect are absent.

Nevertheless, it remains true that a generation seeking upscale employment—in the sense of satisfying, individuated, and highly professional work—is the same generation that is putting greater demands on marriage than any of its predecessors and, when there are children present, is seeking to make relationships with them more satisfying as well. The result may be a superhuman level of demand on both oneself and the other people in one's life. We may be in the process of underestimating the benevolence of habit and routine as a way of making life bearable by making it at least somewhat predictable!

At the risk of quantifying what many readers might regard as ineffable feelings, we would like to suggest a number of thoughts that are helpful in maintaining the distinction between work life and personal life:

> *In the world of work, agreement usually needs to be linear and verbal in order to be effective, while unspoken feelings are likely to be destructive. In a marriage feelings are paramount, and words may be deployed only for purposes of reassurance and repair.*

The world of work is dominated by the idea, or reflex, represented by a contract. Duties and obligations are explicitly spelled out, often in written form. This mode of communication influences every aspect of work life, including the ways in which supervisors regularly speak with their subordinates. Even the boss who is not in the process of giving orders may think through a problem in the presence of a subordinate, meticulously analyzing its implications so that both boss and subordinate tune in to a common fund of knowledge and agree that it is a sound basis for action. A workday spent in analyses of this kind may be regarded with satisfaction by all concerned, and the employees—bosses and subordinates both—may go home with the comfortable feeling that they have more than earned their paychecks. Problems typically arise in business life when concepts, behaviors, and interactions have *not* received sufficient scrutiny and when unarticulated feelings give rise to what may in reality be dangerous decisions.

Marriage, on the other hand, though it may involve a great deal of action and reflection—buying houses and groceries, raising children, visiting relatives, purchasing holiday and birthday presents, pursuing common interests—is based on being rather than becoming. The old phrase "to have and to hold" suggests the sheer proximity that is involved in living in tandem with another person for a period of years and decades. In the business world, just being with someone else can easily be defined as synonymous with loafing. The response to two employees in conversation might well be, "Well, the two of you ought to be *doing* something if this company is to have a future!" But in a marriage, relentless, purposeful activity might well be considered a symptom of something awry within the relationship, which the partners are seeking to bury or control.

> *Within a company, goals are often pursued in a quasi-orgasmic manner. Within a marriage, good sex is symptomatic of a deeper success.*

Many observers have commented on the group rhythm that often typifies business life. The goal may be, for example, to win a lucrative contract or commission. Dozens, even hundreds, of employees may be involved in the total effort required to attain that goal. The ways in which they then proceed to cooperate, the extent to which they bury individual crotchets and preferences in deference to that effort, might very well lead to an admiring article in the pages of *Business Week* or the *Wall Street Journal*. Success, when and if it comes, might lead to a riotous celebration in which employees douse each other with champagne, embrace enthusiastically, and slip off, on occasion, to actually have sex with each other.

Extensive Freudian training is not required to sense that there is an element of erotic fantasy in all of this, as well as a reliving, in various ways, of childhood and even infant emotion. Those with whom one cooperates are good siblings joined in furthering a paternal/maternal corporation. (The very basis of the word corporation is the Latin word *corpus,* which means "body.") The sense of being inside a protective but endangered collectivity may draw on the original experience of enclosure within the womb. Therefore, the corporate rhythm of preparation (foreplay) and achievement (orgasm) is perfectly in keeping with these evocative memories and early experiences.

All of this, however, is sublimated rather than actual sex—quasi-sexual rather than sexual. The office affair, when it occurs, may simply represent the furthest bounds of the fantasy—the moment when it is occasionally acted out.

In a marriage the sexual connection between the partners is primary rather than secondary, real rather than metaphorical, and an embodiment rather than an accompaniment of success. Though a couple may sometimes have sex in order to celebrate a success, sex is more commonly their way of celebrating the marriage.

> *Though parents may represent our first "boss," one of their most important roles is to protect us from bossing.*

The great shift from authoritarian to individuated and cooperative behaviors in business life may reflect the rise in a nurturant rather than authoritarian style of parenting. The bumper sticker reading, "Have you hugged your child today?" would have been regarded as more than mildly subversive in the early years of the twentieth century. The individuated, self-regulating worker had a label waiting for him in the personnel offices of only a few years ago: Troublemaker.

The parent who has spent a day out there in the world of work can be forgiven for feeling some concern about a child's schooling and ability to apply effort in a systematic way. At the same time, few contemporary parents see themselves merely as conduits for the demands being made on their children. In a way that is only sporadically true for a boss in a company, a parent needs to act as a buffer and advocate on behalf of his or her child. The protective function, which in business has an instrumental basis ("If I don't look after those who work for me, I can't expect them to look out for me") is, for a parent, completely self-explanatory. It is a reflexive caring for the child's inner life, and it *incidentally* helps the child to grow up with its core of happiness and security intact—which is the best preparation for adult life.

To sum up, it is possible to love one's work, but work is not about love. It is often necessary to work on behalf of those one loves . . . but that is a different kind of work altogether.

The decentralized/individuated family is a totally new phenomenon in our world. Its rules, which are in fact anti-rules, are still in the process of establishing themselves, and like the more organized and hierarchical patterns that held sway in the childhoods of today's parents, it presents its own blend of risks and satisfactions.

The fears of those who write about disintegration rather than individuation are not completely baseless, however. Spouses with fully developed careers *do* run the risk of growing apart. At the simplest level, they find it relatively easy to arrange extramarital affairs. In a deeper way, their absorption in their jobs can gradually draw their consciousness and their habits away from each other and make the hours at work seem more real, in the end, than the briefer and more weary hours at home.

Similarly, the child who grows up in a decentralized/ individuated family *can* get into trouble. Between day care, school, summer camp, and the full range of parental involvements in activities other than parenting, a child's right to be a full person can shade over into the feeling of neglect. In a single-parent household, the situation may be even more poignant.

Let us assume, however, that these risks are avoided and that a household can be described as individuated rather than disintegrated. How can families then cope with the pressures and stresses posed by our new mode of life, especially if the spouses are both determined to pursue fully developed, demanding careers?

The most significant adaptation that seems to be taking place has to do with standards. As one male executive put it:

> I grew up in a home where you could apply the old adage to my mother's floors: They were clean enough to eat off. Time was pretty relentlessly divided between cooking, cleaning, waxing, polishing, carpet beating, dusting, shopping, and a variety of visits. Life had a military flavor, and there was some nameless retribution that lay in wait—probably at the hands of God himself—for those who had any dirt on their windowsills.
>
> Frankly, I amaze myself when I look around and see that one can actually survive on a different basis. I suppose that having a child played a role here for me, because we had to make a conscious decision as to whether he would be adapted to us or we would adapt to him, and we chose to do the latter. Once in a while we have a guilt attack and do some hard cleaning up, but the tone is mostly pretty loose. Maybe we'll yet get around to hiring a cleaning lady, but so far,

I've managed to make it through a lifetime without one.

We spend time in a flexible way. I don't think that's a formula for instant happiness, by the way. There's something to be said for a more regimented way of life because it keeps your mind away from your problems. On the other hand, there's a lot to be said for knowing what your feelings are. And there's time for exercise and buying fresh as opposed to processed food, which also has a lot to be said for it.

What always strikes me is the amount of time—the percentage of my total week—that I spend in contact and communication with my son. Amid the military schedules that dominated my own childhood, the amount of time spent by my parents in that kind of communication, with me as the focus, was zilch—or a little below zilch. I can see the difference that's made for my son.

I'm not sure whether we're absolutely typical in this respect. A lot of my son's friends seem still to have full-time, stay-at-home mothers. At the same time, they sometimes seem to me to spend excessive amounts of time performing unnecessary acts of supervision.

Though I never thought I'd hear myself say this, I've grown rather attached to the whole fast-food, keep-your-kid-entertained-and-yourself-sane industry. I no longer critique it as being vulgar or unhealthy when compared with a four-star restaurant where the steaks arrive smothered in cholesterol sauce. And I'll even manage to sit through movies like *The Muppets Take Manhattan* and *Return of the Jedi* that aren't going to put William Styron out of business. Best of all, the kid's old enough now to go into one movie at the

> seven- or nine-theater complex while I go into another.
>
> Yes, I do still have attacks in which it seems temporarily clear to me that I should be living in a fancier, cleaner, neater house like the ones they still feature in Hollywood movies—unless the occupant is a single male, at which point they arrange some antiseptic "mess." I suppose I'll have those for the rest of my life. As the Jesuits used to say, "Give us the boy until the age of six, and we will cheerfully relinquish him thereafter." Maybe the generations still to come will make a more sublime adaptation. But compared to the life I grew up with, this one looks pretty good!

What people seem to be doing in today's world is putting an emphasis on upscale time as well as on upscale relationships and an upscale work life. Each of these, in turn, can be defined by its flexibility—its lack of rigidity and constrained role playing. In this sense, the looser patterns pioneered in the 1960s can be said to have continued their spread while many of the more radical 1960s activities have been discontinued or reversed. Superficial conformity today often masks an underlying restlessness and a willingness to take risks, as when a young executive who dresses for success also switches jobs at the drop of a hat if there seems to be more opportunity and more stimulation available elsewhere. Time has become a sinuous, rather than a fixed and limited, commodity.

The sense that we live in a stressful time and the sense that many fixed signposts have vanished from our lives are two sides of the same coin. If fixed, rigid roles are less and less visible in work life and in personal life, then people are finding themselves in the middle of an unprecedented process that could be described as continual, even continuous, negotiation.

Couples go to therapists because they see a chance of renegotiating the terms of their relationship in a way that may keep it from dissolving altogether. Canny supervisors in the workplace monitor the satisfaction level of a valued subordinate and are prepared for careful discussion on the subject of how things might be done differently. Faced with one of today's super-aware children, a parent may feel as if he or she were, in fact, a United Nations official in a perpetual search for words and formulas that will restore some corner of the world to relative stability.

What this means is that the very substance of our lives has undergone a remarkable change. Activities that were once peripheral now represent how we spend most of our time. The formerly necessary has become relatively marginal. And the most critical word in our vocabularies has become "development," with its suggestion that life is synonomous with change.

This is not just a national, but an international, phenomenon. It helps to explain the fluid, endlessly dynamic economy that ties the nations of the globe together while making them feel, at the same time, perpetually threatened by their competition. In economic life as in family life, we are growing used to the exhilarating and terrifying awareness that there is no Big Daddy or Mommy, no final and omniscient Authority, to tell us what we should be doing with ourselves. The marketplace is only a partial substitute for that earlier fantasy—and may turn out to be a temporary one.

Increasingly, we live in a world of equals who wake up each morning with a flexible agenda and who can experience neither the pleasure nor the pain of taking things for granted.

Part Three

The best lack all conviction, while the worst
Are full of passionate intensity.
—*William Butler Yeats*

Fate chooses our relatives, we choose our friends.

—Jacques DeLille

The New Intimacy

Even if we define a lot of what is going on today as decentralization rather than disintegration, the fact is that life in a looser, more option-filled society tends to generate a search for cohesion. The need for order and for a sense of belonging is one that will return even if people do prize the freedoms and choices that the modern world has given them.

This, in turn, helps to explain the organization of so much of modern life around the workplace. This can be called *a search for salvation through work,* and it obviously has deep psychological roots in the minds of individual employees. It contrasts in obvious ways with the hippie attitudes briefly fashionable in the late 1960s and early 1970s that implied that mental states, reachable through meditation or drugs, took precedence over any kind of organized activity or goal-oriented pursuit.

The fierce identification with business in general and with particular companies that has characterized the late 1970s and the 1980s is occasionally pointed to as a resurgence of the Protestant work ethic, implying that what happened in the 1960s or at some earlier point in the twentieth century represented a break in the historical thread running back to Luther and Calvin. People used to gather together to work very hard, runs this particular myth, but then somehow we all got spoiled, and what we need to do now is to relearn the joys of committed labor—which is what our noblest young people are in the process of doing.

But as Paul Bernstein pointed out five years ago in *The Wharton Magazine,* citing the work of sociologist Sebastian De Grazia,

> Workers in the centuries after Luther and Calvin never fully subscribed to the work ethic. Work was a means to an end. One worked to earn a living, not because of religious duty.
>
> It is useless to rail against the decline of a work ethic that never had the universal support attributed to it. It is unproductive to compare the contemporary worker with an idealized counterpart of yesteryear, particularly since there is no clear evidence that the passage of time has created a work force that is less motivated than its predecessors.
>
> There is a *new* work ethic abroad in America. It is unrelated to religious demands of ministers and manufacturers' representatives, but is part and parcel of the individual desire for meaningful and challenging labor in which some autonomy is an integral feature.

The new American work ethic can be seen as an inevitable accompaniment to the rise of individuation as a strong shared value. At the same time, identification with the corporate aspect of work life—using "corporate" in several senses of the word—may also answer some of the emotional needs that individuation has brought with it.

The first step toward our new mass individuation was, as we have already noted, the middle-class exodus to the suburbs after World War II—one of the greatest social movements in the history of the world. Millions upon millions of Americans suddenly found it perfectly plausible to leave behind the old city neighborhood with its ethnic homogeneities, its relatively extended families, and its relatively rigorous social conformity. While the world was "opening up" for them in economic terms, they were contracting it in terms of the sphere to which they wanted to pay attention before and after work—narrowing that sphere to what we now call the "nuclear family."

It was in suburban families of this kind that the next generation was produced: one in which the sense of self and the need for self-respect and self-worth took precedence over marriage and family. In turn, this *even* more individuated generation, when it produced children at all, gave birth to today's preteens: ten- and eleven-year-olds who drop casual comments on oral sex, AIDS, and their single parent's current boyfriend or girlfriend.

Individuation, it appears, can go no further. The children of former screen idols write memoirs revealing to the world what rats they were raised by. Best-selling novels portray the governments of the world, including our own, as riddled with conspiracy and corruption, with the agencies in charge of security being the ones most likely to harbor the spies trained by the other side. And those same novels sometimes find themselves echoed on the front pages of *The New York Times* and the *Washington Post.*

In a society so pervasively loosened, with new fractures sprouting while the old ones widen, two social phenomena stand out as mass reactions in the opposite direction: the "new patriotism" that soared to ever-growing heights of media coverage in 1986 and the romanticization of work and careers that was a steady theme in American life even before the 1980s were born.

Part of the new ethic of individuation is a distaste for passivity and the conviction that one can, with a bit of willpower, *make a difference*. In this sense, the young people of the mid-1980s are not unrelated to the rebel activists of the sixties and early seventies. In addition to those who are still engaged in traditional or newly created types of consciousness-raising—including shelters for the homeless, preservation of the environment, or an end to Apartheid—there are a much larger number who channel their crusading energies into marketing and sales, either on behalf of a company that employs them or on behalf of themselves as independents.

In the world of the 1960s, it was possible for Abbie Hoffman, Jerry Rubin, and Mario Savio to portray American business—and money-making in general—as a conspiracy against justice and decency because business could obviously do whatever it wanted, including manufacturing napalm and its delivery systems. Once the vulnerability of American business had been graphically demonstrated by the Arab oil embargo and our German and East Asian competitors, the time was ripe for quasi-religious figures like Lee Iacocca and Peter Uebberroth who, supported by President Reagan, preached the ability of the "can-do" American spirit to cope with even the most formidable obstacles. Highly motivated individuals could cope with sluggish companies, they declared. Highly motivated companies could cope with sluggish industries. A highly motivated America could revive the spirit that, a hundred years earlier, had made it great.

For those who try to carry this new spirit of dedication into a traditional company setting, there are some special risks. One of these is the heightened willingness of companies to fire their white-collar personnel, including junior and senior executives, in an economic crunch. There are Fortune 500 corporations that regularly weed out 20 percent of their white-collar workers, even when no financial crisis has struck, on the grounds that it "keeps the others lively."

Another serious risk for the idealistic employee in a corporate setting is the possibility of being victimized by what is often referred to as "group process" or "group dynamics." Companies and corporations represent one version of a phenomenon that has received more and more attention in recent years: the human tendency to form groups, and the cycle that all groups tend to have in common. In order to study this phenomenon, academic researchers observe small groups of people who gather together on a regular basis and define themselves as a group. (Often, these are people who have registered for a course in group dynamics!)

What these researchers often report, after studying videotapes and audio recordings, is an archetypal group cycle that begins with feelings of strength and purpose, metamorphoses slowly into doubt and disaffection, and leads finally to a crisis that culminates, usually, in the deposition of the group leader. This is typically followed by a period of regret and mourning in which the decision to terminate the leader is questioned and regretted. Then the leader is invited to reassume his or her position, or an entirely new leader is selected, and the cycle begins all over again.

Studies of this kind have helped to illuminate many social and political processes, especially those in which a leader enjoys an unrealistic honeymoon period, then loses popularity (sometimes to the point of proposed impeachment), and ultimately regains stature and power by launching a dramatic campaign of some kind. At the national level, this can mean going to war. At the corporate level, it might mean the launching of a completely new product.

In group life of all kinds, in other words, there is a death-and-resurrection cycle that is regularly played out, one that involves not only the leader but also his or her followers. When the group as a whole feels itself moving into a crisis and begins to question the leader's competence and authority, the leader can deflect these feelings of hostility by turning them outward against a common enemy (which may be another country or another company), by shifting the blame to an internal scapegoat, or in some cases by committing actual or symbolic suicide. The group cycle thus helps to illuminate the ancient pattern, commemorated in Mary Renault's novel *The King Must Die,* whereby the most important person in a society has often also been designated as a sacrificial victim.

For those who enthusiastically identify their career progress with the furthering of a company's welfare and profits, this line of research offers a number of cautions. Crusades, though they are directed at outside competition, can also be turned against some of those who willingly embark on them. Moreover, the cycle through which companies, like other groups, tend to pass are at least as heavily determined by internal, individual psychology as they are by the objective facts of the marketplace. That is why major companies go through dramatic episodes in which they act incredibly dumb and disorganized, with disastrous consequences for all concerned, followed, after the sacrifice of some corporate officers, by reorganization and a period of sustained, triumphant prosperity.

For the individual highly committed professional, awareness of group dynamics enables some appropriate cautions to be exercised. Above all, it enables the employee to keep firmly in mind that the company is a creation within the minds of those who staff it, in much the same way that a government is sustained by those who regard themselves as having allegiance to it. In each case we are dealing with a compelling fiction. In turn, those who accept the fiction, or deeply believe in it, are sometimes capable of behavior that can spell danger for some of their fellows. Unjust scapegoatings and firings, in a corporate context, may be the response to a group crisis and may be passively or actively accepted by the victim's coworkers who seemed friendly and warm only a few days before. In the world of politics, particularly when it involves an unstable society, the consequences can be much more unpleasant.

The risks posed by the group cycle are especially severe for the person who gets entirely or substantially swept away by corporate existence. The enthusiast, whose committed energies bring all kinds of praise when people are feeling generally up, may find himself or herself deeply hurt—even crushed—when a sacrificial lamb is required, and he or she is *it*.

In this context, it may be helpful to reflect on how recently the very concept of a corporation was enshrined in the laws of industrial nations. Until the end of the nineteenth century, most people felt that if an individual formed a business venture of any kind, singlehandedly or with other people, then the responsibility for the consequences of that venture also had to take an individual form. When the concept of the corporation was developed and fully legalized, those who carried through the revolution understood that they were creating a fiction whose purpose it was to separate personal from business liability so that commercial activities could be carried out more freely and effectively, without perpetual fear of personal financial ruin.

But since that time the whole effort of corporations in their marketing and advertising activities has been to create an identity—a collective personality—that is turned outward toward customers and inward toward employees. In this way the legal fiction can become a kind of psychological presence. In the mind of the worker, "the company" begins to live as if it were, in fact, a human being. It is only a short step from there to the feeling that "it" ranks with one's parents, spouse, and children in the hierarchy of human values.

The fact that a fantasy of this kind is widely shared and may even, to a certain extent, be irresistible, is all the more reason for keeping watch on one's own feelings. The day you find yourself referring to the fiction that employs you as if it were a parent, spouse, lover, or child is the day you know you are in danger of making some very bad mistakes!

The impact of group life within companies is particularly visible in the area of mutual resentment, more accurately known as envy. There are psychologists and philosophers who maintain that our society is riddled with envy. Everyone seems to be engaged in resenting those with bigger houses, better cars, or a more attractive appearance. And since there is no definable top or bottom to the social and financial pyramid, even good-looking millionaires turn green when they contemplate the property and appearance of those with yet more wealth, more beauty.

The eternal image of the envious person is that of someone standing outside a window or at the periphery of a crowd, watching another person or group of people having a wonderfully happy time. The envious person feels the anguish of rejection because *they* (whoever "they" happen to be) are basking in warmth, wealth, and acceptance while he or she is literally or symbolically out in the cold.

This suggests the power that envy exercises in a context like the business world, where quantification in terms of salaries, perks, and office location is so relentless. Large companies are explicitly set up as pecking orders so that executives and employees envy those with bigger windows and better carpeting—or those who have windows and carpeting at all! Meanwhile, companies organize a pecking order among themselves in which those with larger amounts of capital, better distribution networks, or superior repair records can send out appropriate signals of condescension to those still mired in problems or those comparatively minuscule in size.

Envy has been compared to the proverbial "fire under one's ass." It leads people to try hard, and harder still, in their struggle to catch up, even though there is no level imaginable at which additional catch-up may not be required.

Though the workings of envy are omnipresent in business life, they pose an additional risk at a time when being a financially successful professional has taken on some of the meaning once attributed to grace in Christian theology. In effect, the ranks of the successful have come to be conceived as a kind of bandwagon, the exclusion from which is a sign of personal unworthiness or active culpability. While sentiments like that can be injurious in business and professional life by suggesting that a financial reverse is also a moral reverse, they can be positively destructive in the world of personal relations.

Here are three relevant anecdotes we have gathered from persons now in their late thirties or early forties:

The Story of John

John is a reasonably successful professor of English at a respectable private university that still falls short of Ivy League status. His books and articles have been well received. He has tenure, and his job would be in peril only if the university itself were to move into financial crisis, which is a possibility that cannot be ruled out at a time when there are fewer and fewer high-school seniors preparing to graduate and move on to college—the famous "shrinking demographics" that will not end until the 1990s. He observes,

Looking back on my first marriage, I'm struck by how much of it was determined by envy, which was and is the emotion that has played the powerhouse role in my life. My wife and I met while we were still undergraduates, and then embarked, in effect, on parallel careers. Almost without realizing it, we were soon measuring our accomplishments against each other's. I can still remember the day we got our acceptance letters to graduate school. I was offered a couple of first-rate fellowships at Ivy League schools. She received some good admissions with no financial aid. She had what amounted to a mini–nervous breakdown, during which she broke things in the kitchen for a while and generally just screamed and cried. It wasn't directed *at* me, but it was certainly prompted *by* my situation.

That episode, in turn, pointed to a later one that made an equally strong impression on me—even stronger, in some ways. I had just completed my dissertation defense. The university had a policy under which they published the one dissertation each year that won the something-or-other prize. My wife met me as I was leaving the building in which my defense had taken place, and she asked me with a certain ambiguous eagerness whether I had won the prize. When I said that I hadn't, though the dissertation had been approved with very minor revisions, there crossed her face a fleeting but unmistakable look of satisfaction.

We've been divorced for many years now, but I have the sense that the competition will really end only with the grave. In some weird way, she's *still* trying to prove something to me . . . that her life has worked out better, that she's happier than I am, and that all her decisions have been appropriate ones. And I've gotten in my own digs as part of the horrible process.

It's probably relevant that both of us came from backgrounds in which there was some significant emotional deprivation in early life. That seems to set the stage for this kind of envy-ridden existence in later years, with the nose eternally pressed at an imaginary sweetshop window whose goodies are always just out of reach. I think that's just the worst feeling in the world. I wish I had a surefire formula for getting out from under it.

The Story of Kathleen

As a newsletter editor in New York City, who subsequently moved into selling real estate, Kathleen experienced the traumatic life of an employee in a small company run by an intensely narcissistic boss:

In a funny or obvious kind of way, the cohesion and relative friendliness of the employees was based on the incredible ways in which our boss tried to make you feel that you weren't as favored by the gods as he was. He started out, when I first went to work for him, being rather good at flattering you and finding ways to get you to work hard. Then the long slide began. Like other narcissists I've run into, his general tone was that *he* was infallible but surrounded, for some strange reason, by pathetic incompetents. One of his specialties was to raise the subscription price of your newsletter beyond what the market could bear and then to blame the resulting drop in subscriptions on *your* editorial work. When the whole shebang began to deteriorate into outright sadism and abuse, I got out. I make less money now, but I'm completely self-employed, and I don't have to put up with chattel slavery masquerading as a job.

Frankly, I think this was a guy whose desire to have you envy *him* was based on the fact that he was so badly envying *you*. If you were competent and also liked by your fellow employees, I think he ended up by really eating his heart out. I've never had such an oppressive awareness of hierarchy in a work situation, where the smallest touch could be used against you. Watching this particular person go downhill was like being caught up in a badly written tragedy.

The Story of Harold

"I knew Harold when we were both undergraduates," observed a middle-aged executive in a New England company that manufactures computer-related equipment,

> but I only began to envy him when he moved up rapidly in a corporation closely related to my own. Our contacts were superficially friendly, but I always felt that he was really completely uninterested in the details of my life and expected conversation to center on the supremely fascinating subject known as *his* life. He was, and I suppose still is, an excellent politician.
>
> You can see how distorted my thinking became when I say that it took me longer than most people to become aware of the extent to which his career has gotten stuck. A lot of people seem to be walking around with the feeling that he has rubbed their noses in the dirt. Those who work for him often bad-mouth him in ways that get around. His divorce was about as painful as anybody else's—and maybe an inordinately large blow to his ego.

> I've done a lot of thinking about Harold, and the conclusion I've reached is that with all of his energy, he's mainly a disintegrative force on those around him. He gets *things* done, but at a high cost in the long-range effect on those around him. His flair for showmanship can't compensate for the suspicion that folks have about the price an organization pays when he is heading it up.

If heightened feelings of envy reflect one side of today's company orientation, the other can be summed up as a form of intimacy, of deep bonding, that traditional family life cannot match. "When Job and Life Merge, Many Ignore the Clock," ran the title of an article that appeared in the *Hartford Courant* on February 25, 1986, while the headline on a continuation page read, "For Achievers, 40 Hours Isn't Enough." The article described, among other people, an advertising executive who recalled the time before his divorce. "I did a little presentation for my wife and kids," the executive recalled. "I used an easel and explained to them what I was going to have to do over the next six weeks and how much time it was going to take and how I wouldn't be home all that much."

Though the article took no note of the fact, the ad-man was, in fact, treating his family like a *client*. In a similarly disconnected manner, the author of the article observed many paragraphs later, "In many professions—advertising, journalism, law, architecture, banking—the nature of the job requires more than the usual forty hours. And that often means socializing with the people you share office time with." The ad-man who gave the lecture to his family, complete with easel, was then quoted as saying, "When you work in a stimulating atmosphere and survive the pressures, people tend to have an affinity toward one another. You do hang out together."

The family as client; the company as family. For

today's workbound professional, the satisfactions of the office can run the full gamut from parenting to being parented, and from sibling bonds and rivalries to what we have dubbed the Theseus/Hippolyta Syndrome.

Theseus, king of Athens, sailed to the Black Sea on one of his adventures and there found the great love of his life, the Amazon Hippolyta. After he had beaten her in single combat, he brought her back to Athens, and they became companions not only in bed but on the battlefield. She died, finally, by taking an arrow meant for him.

This ancient fantasy of a loving man and a manlike woman sharing the perils of war and deepening their relationship in combat is one that frequently gets resurrected in today's workplace, as a man and a woman get to know each other's minds and emotions amid daily scenes of stress and financial risk. The bonds forged through a process of this kind can make those of a marriage seem pale by comparison, especially when a dual-career couple arrives home too late to share a dinner and too tired even to think about the office.

Here is an account provided to us by a journalist who works at a major American newspaper:

> The sheer daily thrill is what keeps me in this otherwise crazy profession, and it's never been quite as intense as when I started to work on a cooperative basis with another reporter, whom I'll call Joanne. The lock-in between us was so intense—and we pulled each other out of so many tight spots in the first year or two of our work together—that the relationship had taken on sexual or quasi-marital overtones even before she invited me to go to bed with her. The fact that she had every intention of staying married probably doomed the affair from the start—that and some of the problems the paper started to have

> once a new and incompetent publisher was brought on board. But for a while, it was perfect. We'd go to a motel, share a picnic-type lunch with wine, talk shop, have sex, talk personal life, have some more sex, and talk shop again as we were winding down.

The fact is that today's office, more than today's family, resembles the family situation that was normative in most societies well into the nineteenth and even the twentieth century. At a time when families survived economically through the careful exploitation of a family farm or workshop, each new child quickly became a "hand." The tightness and interdependency of the family grew out of the fact that each member was both a drain and a contributor. Relationships were structured in such a way as to make the contribution maximal and the drain as small as possible.

In families like that, the father was truly an authority and the mother truly a provider. In the absence of hospitals and even physicians, the latter was one of the few lifesavers around. Meanwhile, the brutality, by our standards, of the average father took place in a world where survival was always precarious and death just around the corner.

Our own families have become more nurturant and less psychologically damaging at the point in history when they have also become less absolutely *necessary*. Divorce is thinkable today only because it threatens the finances, rather than the lives, of those who embark on it.

Paradoxically, therefore, it is the ever-vulnerable company that has tended to fill the void left behind as the governments of industrialized nations provide the social and economic cushions formerly available only within the family setting. Here the sense of people pulling together and sacrificing individual comforts and quirks in the interest of a larger commonality has continued to live and flourish.

There is, of course, a difference. The threats perceived in a company setting, and the efforts then mobilized to meet them, can hardly be compared with the struggle to get the harvest in and thereby avert actual starvation. But adrenaline can be set pumping in a metaphorical as well as an actual situation. The language generated in company settings, and the emotions triggered by it in the hearts of employees, has all of the urgency and campaign mentality of that used at harvest time before the Industrial Revolution and on the battlefields of Waterloo and The Marne. The adrenaline may be even higher where the self-employed entrepreneur is concerned, whose sixteen- or eighteen-hour workday cannot be slowed down by the reflection that "it's not my money."

In today's workplace, the enthusiasm and group élan summed up by the word *campaign* is available at a time when many other areas of life have become increasingly predictable. In turn, the sense of group striving is a powerful cement between those who share the stresses of the campaign in ways that can take on sexual overtones or even lead to actual physical intimacy; the result may be a drain on the libido that is available within the environment of the home.

Gone are the days when work, however many hours it lasted, was mainly physical. Gone, too, are the days when white-collar work consisted primarily of routine tasks. Increasingly, the demands of the workplace are qualitative as well as quantitative. The sheer pace of competition in the modern world sees to it that workers are thinking, or trying to think, new thoughts all the time, to function in an entrepreneurial and innovative manner even when their job titles sound quite routine.

For more and more people, therefore, the process of coming down from a day of work has come to be a job in itself. Here are the reflections of the head of a communications group that has only recently been launched in a New England city:

> The most striking thing about my workday is that when it's over, I don't even know what it has done to me! Phase one of my evening is the drive home, which is brief and neither taxing nor relaxing. Then comes a lie-down with some taped classical music, which usually leads to an hour or so of sleep. *Then* I begin to realize how tired I am, but also how cramped-up and tense. After dinner, I drive to a local community center, usually with my son in tow, for a half hour of swimming, which helps me to work out the cramps. Meanwhile, my son works out in the gym. I get home just in time to hit the sack. No TV, no puttering about, no extended conversation. Just *sleep*.

A schedule of this kind—and these comments are from someone who seldom works later than five or five-thirty—sees to it that all available energy is expended on job-related functions and that even such necessary chores as paying bills and taking out the garbage have to be budgeted for if they are to be performed at all.

The fact that so many people are now immersed in their work lives with this degree of intensity also helps to explain the relative loss of interest in sex that has been commented on ever since the 1980s began ("the new chastity"). The shift of libido into workplace functions—what Freud termed *sublimation*—has been detrimental to many relationships, especially those which, because they are long-term, have lost their initial charge of passion.

For those seeking to balance out their lives, affairs with coworkers or those encountered in business situations may seem attractive in comparison. They often take place during the day, on company time, and at a point when energies are still running high. They omit, by definition, all the draggy realities of dishes, vacuuming, and child care that, after a full day of intoxicated labor, can represent the coup de grace to one's libido.

But the arrival of a new demographic era may restore balance in a larger sense by making labor scarce and encouraging individuals—with the willing or unwilling cooperation of their employers—to redefine the balance between work and the other aspects of life.

Even if many Americans work fewer and/or more flexible hours, lower productivity may not necessarily be the result. In Japan, for example, land of legendary twelve-hour days and seven-day weeks, productivity gains are now being accomplished through high technology rather than unwearying human labor. At the same time, there are signs that today's Japanese executive is seeking a less work-obsessed, more family-centered life.

Even if many Americans work fewer hours, there may be gains for the economy if they work more cooperatively, in a way that synthesizes entrepreneurial values with the social outlook that has been derided in recent years as "liberal" or "left-wing." They may eventually meet their Japanese counterparts in the territory midway between extremes, where work and personal life are seen as complementary values.

Annual income twenty pounds, annual expenditure nineteen nineteen six, result happiness. Annual income twenty pounds, annual expenditure twenty pounds ought and six, result misery.
—*Charles Dickens*

Homo Economicus: The Interplay of Reason and Terror

The workaholic syndrome is based, obviously, on a prodigal output of energy. Energy, in turn, can flow from a variety of sources, including joy and terror.

Much of what we have described so far in this book emphasizes the role of work as an organizing force in the life of today's American, a source of meaning so intense that it can actually substitute for the values of love and family. To round off this assessment, however, it is necessary for us to take into account an aspect of American thinking and feeling that is centered on the subject of money and that helps to explain the spread of workaholic behavior in the United States today.

The meaning that money has for us as individuals has always been a difficult subject to discuss because of the way in which money combines an extreme surface rationality with deep underlying anxiety and *ir*rationality. The best-known example is probably the psychoanalytic association between money and feces. But even in daily life we can see many examples of the way in which the rational pursuit of money—as that which enables one to obtain a variety of needs and satisfactions—becomes intermixed with some intensely irrational motivations.

Even if the Latin phrase is seldom used, those who enter the world of financial planning are familiar with the concept of the *Homo economicus*, the human being driven solely by considerations of financial gain or loss. A human being of this kind is obviously not subject to uncertainty, ambiguity, or ambivalence. Having defined his or her life as the completely rational pursuit of a universally agreed-upon good, he or she can then measure success in a completely objective way: the more money one is worth, the more one has succeeded.

In practice, of course, *Homo economicus* seldom comes out looking this unruffled. For example, if money is in fact being pursued for rational ends—to provide personal needs and satisfactions—then there ought to be a nearly complete taboo on seeking it in ways and styles that impact negatively on one's physical health. (A body in poor shape is not the ideal vehicle for satisfaction.) Even those seeking much larger amounts of money than are necessary for a high level of personal satisfaction ought still to be safeguarding their physical well-being if only to be in optimum shape for the *contemplation* of their wealth.

Above all, those who are rationally pursuing the good thing called money ought to be relatively free of anxiety and status uncertainty. The more money you have, the safer you are from such disasters as hunger, homelessness, or reliance on welfare. The higher your percentile within the hierarchy of American incomes, the more objectively you have established your own importance and the calmer you ought to be.

If reality seldom works this way, and money is often seen as "anxiety in action" within the life of the individual, then we may have to look elsewhere for an understanding of its contribution to the workaholic syndrome.

We might well begin by looking at *religion*—not the formal kind that is associated with church or synagogue membership but the more important kind that, over hundreds of years, has shaped the assumptions of even those Americans who regard themselves as agnostics or atheists. Specifically, we need to look at America as a Calvinistic society whose attitudes toward work and money express some of the powerful paradoxes that have made Calvinism an influential social and economic force among people and societies of North European origin.

The Protestant and Calvinistic point of view, we all learn at school, was a shift in emphasis from "works" to "faith" as the basis for salvation in the afterlife. Reformation Protestants agreed with Catholics that only a limited number of human beings could hope to escape the torments of Hell. Whereas Catholics maintained that actions performed in this world could reduce or eliminate the time spent in Purgatory and prevent the eternal sentence to Hell, the new breed of Protestants maintained that God could not be circumscribed or directed by the actions of mere mortals, that His choices and decisions were inscrutable, and that even faith was a symptom rather than a cause of salvation. The fact that a man or woman led a blameless and industrious life and prospered economically suggested that he or she was filled with the awareness of having been chosen by God to join His elect and to avoid the fate of eternal damnation.

Protestant and Calvinist reasoning of this kind led to the development of a whole genre of writing—the redemption narrative—in which a sinner suddenly becomes conscious of God's grace and undergoes an abrupt transition from the status of lost soul to that of evangelical preacher. (The classic example is John Bunyan's *Grace Abounding to the Chief of Sinners.*) What all of these narratives have in common, and what could be called the archetypal Protestant experience, is the sudden awareness of one's personality being flooded with grace, accompanied by an equally sudden change in behavior in which dissipation gives way to industry, foul-mouthedness to preaching, and the constant threat of penury to the virtues of productivity and thrift.

Long after most Americans had lost the ability to paraphrase any of Luther's or Calvin's ideas, the notion that worldly success is a symptom of virtue was to play a growing role in American life. Today, that role is expressed in a succinct phrase that appears on many of the novelties sold by American retailers: "Poverty Sucks." The idea clearly implied by this dictum is that the *poor* suck—or in Reformation language, bear witness to the fact that they are among the damned. Hence the truly religious power of the American assumption, often articulated by Ronald Reagan, that *any* poor person can pull himself up by his own bootstraps if only he experiences the moment of conversion that enables him to mobilize his energies and the American "can-do" spirit. Figures like Lee Iacocca and Peter Ueberroth play a role in the American imagination that is very much like that of the traditional Protestant hero, for whom the overcoming of horrendous obstacles and the achievement of glorious goals *is* religion.

In this sense, *Homo economicus* is a person for whom absolute rationality in the accomplishment of worldly tasks is a rigorously mandated and anxiety-laden religious mission. Remember that for Calvin and the other Protestant reformers, those chosen by God for redemption—the "saved" or "elect"—were and always would be a tiny percentage of the human race. Everyone else was predestined for eternal damnation. In turn, the accoutrements of respectability that testified to one's inner conviction of being among the elect, known as "faith," acquired a level of theological importance—including the house one owned, the dishes off which one ate, and the clothing one wore. The typically middle-class objects that are so lovingly painted in Dutch art of the sixteenth and seventeenth centuries are the exact equivalent, in other words, of the expensive objects that a modern-day Yuppie might purchase at Bloomingdale's. *Having them, and having the ability to buy them, testifies to the fact that you are okay and not among the damned.*

America's Calvinist heritage helps to explain America's equally deep commitment to Social Darwinism. Once the poor and incompetent have been identified as those whose lack of faith ranks them among the damned, it seems quite natural that the help they receive from government, such as it is, should be administered in a degrading manner. That, in turn, lights a fire under the posteriors of Americans who work very hard and invest their money very industriously to avoid what often does look like a fate worse than death—humiliating survival.

Though Calvinism originated in Europe, it is in the United States that it continues to function as a major source of societal "glue." Europeans tend to be horrified by the extent to which members of the American underclass are treated as outcasts. They also tend to be impressed by what they interpret as the energy, dynamism, creativity, or vitality of American society: its sheer capacity for boundless innovation. These two aspects of American national character are closely related. Terror of being "out" leads to boundless energy in the service of being among those who are "in"—the elect or saved who take such pleasure in each other's company as they assure each other of their fully redeemed status.

One result of this shared national ethos is the image, in literature and art, of America as a race to nowhere. For even if *Time*, *Newsweek*, and the *Wall Street Journal* all agree that one is "hot" or "in," the individual knows all too well how easily that could change. A shift in fad or fashion can leave even the most powerful reputation high and dry. A prolonged catastrophic illness can wipe out assets that once seemed invulnerable. For Americans, the safety nets taken for granted in a European society are less available. Hence the ambivalent fascination with which Americans devour newspaper stories about, for example, elderly women who are forced to sue their invalid and hospitalized husbands for support. (Only a court order can clear the legal underbrush that would otherwise require them to be completely destitute before they receive any welfare payments.)

In short, Americans share a language and a set of cultural assumptions in which self-fulfillment and rational financial planning are accompanied by secret terror. Though this does not sound like a very attractive frame of mind when callously stated on the printed page, it helps to explain the drama and excitement of life between the Atlantic and the Pacific, including the current idolization of anything that can be termed "entrepreneurial." The entrepreneur is the man or woman who most fully accepts the shared, though mostly unspoken, rules by which Americans live. And just as theologians once referred to "the risk of faith"—the inner leap that was required before one could throw oneself into the arms of an inscrutable God—so the successful entrepreneur is presented to us by the media, or in a speech by the president of the United States, as a person courageous enough to fling himself or herself into the void of possibility and to parachute into glorious success.

Calvinism has rooted itself so deeply in the American value system, in other words, because it is so compatible with melodrama, including the versions of melodrama peddled by Hollywood, TV, the newsmagazines, and the daily papers. When the alternatives are perceived as beatific salvation and complete eternal failure, life takes on a sharp, even lurid, character. The workaholic character looks, in this context, like a perfectly logical response to something so desperately important.

What is virtually eliminated from consideration, however, is average daily existence and reasonable, predictable behaviors. The vision of personal life that increasingly dominates our assumptions could be compared to zero-base budgeting, in which a corporate cost center, at the end of each fiscal year, has to justify every penny of the budget it is requesting for the next fiscal year. The individual, in this new vision, has to begin each new *day* at an imaginary zero-level. His or her worth needs to be proved all over again under the conditions that obtain *right now* in our fast-moving, ever-changing world. Confidence with respect to one's salvation has to be earned over and over and over again.

All of this helps to account for the fact that the modern American *Homo economicus* never does reach a point of rational satisfaction and lives, in effect, a life without limits in which anxiety-levels increase rather than diminish as financial involvements multiply.

But a life without limits—a life of unlimited striving—is possible only for those who have youth, health, and energy on their side, and for whom limitation is not a psychological necessity. Even in the United States, that leaves a lot of people unaccounted for. For them, the question is: How can I define a satisfying life for myself outside or alongside the topless mountain we climb in the search for financial success and recognized status? What it feels like to struggle with this question is suggested by the words of an accomplished and widely published, though far from wealthy, writer:

One of the things that always amazes me is when people whose opinion I trust tell me that I am widely envied. I spend so much time envying others—for the size of their houses and their offices, the money in their bank accounts and the presumed happiness they enjoy in their BMW's and Corvettes—that I lose sight of the possibility that they may be having similar feelings in *my* direction.

Oddly enough, or maybe not so oddly, my theoretical lust for wealth doesn't lead me to make the effort that's needed to actually accumulate it. In a way that I usually characterize as self-indulgent, I prefer to spend my time engrossed in thought and working out a variety of concepts and problems. I go off in all kinds of tangents and directions, which have in common only the fact that they are mine. I spend a lot of time concentrating on thoughts that are, frankly, quite upsetting, or that cause me at least some discomfort. In a sense, I'm performing an act of personal therapy at the same time that I explore a subject that might lead to an article or a lecture.

When the time does come and I'm asked to produce, I find that I can do so in a relatively effortless way. Because I'm so used to following my own bent and reasoning things through in a completely personal manner, my powers of concentration aren't in any way impeded or drained. I can perform at a high level even when I'm physically very tired, didn't sleep well, or whatever.

The problem, alas, is that I have such trouble in accepting the trade-off. I want to be admired for what I can do. At the same time, I want the rewards that accrue to those with quite a different way of life. My *want* system is out of order.

> That's why I have been so interested in listening to you on the subject of the search for limits. I do find that my personal incapacity to define appropriate limits for myself, and a capacity for satisfaction, has been intensified by the American milieu. I look back on a life in the course of which I've pretty much done whatever I wanted, and I can't rouse up an appropriate feeling of gratitude!

The speaker here is an uncommonly reflective—and self-reflective—individual, but his thoughts shed light on what we have found to be the case in many conversations with intelligent and accomplished men and women. Though they define their struggles as striving for success, what they actually seem to be hungering for is stability, which can be defined as a balance between the inside and outside worlds. That, in turn, implies an ability to *strike* such a balance, which is only possible when you stop piling on more and more.

Here are some reflections by a psychologist who has published a number of articles on the subject of American national character:

> Even after the economic traumas of the 1970s and 1980s, I'm not sure Americans have shed the deep impression that you can keep expanding into a limitless universe and that you never have to make do with a limited amount of anything. Keeping that faith alive may be one reason that the space program has retained so much popularity and that Americans are so shocked when it turns out to be "only human" and kills some of its astronauts.
>
> Historically, Americans have always looked with interest or envy on European or Japanese cultures that were forced to achieve within severe material or geographical constraints, like Mich-

> elangelo figuring out how to carve his statue of David from a block of marble that another sculptor had already ruined. In contrast, Americans tend to favor the notion that you can always find a hundred sculptors to make you a thousand Davids once you've got enough capital to buy them a thousand perfect blocks of marble—and you can write the purchase price off when it comes time for your company to pay its taxes! That kind of an outlook is sprawling, amorphous, dynamic, undefined—and very stressful on the individual psyche. It's not punctuated with enough moments of rest, when you step back from an artistic or technological achievement—Michelangelo's David, or that marvelous dam the Dutch built across the Zuider Zee—and cry, "Bravo!"
>
> But the relentless quest for more is one that's encouraged by the very nature of the international economy today, in which all countries are racing all the time to see which one reaches the next peak in consumer electronics or industrial robotics or what-have-you. The picture I sometimes get is that of a whole planet of football-team workaholics, with presidents and prime ministers as coaches, and self-flagellation in the post-game session each time you and all of your fellow citizens "lose."

Indeed, we have found that this type of football-team mentality, complete with references to our national opponents, the Japanese and Germans, has become pervasive in public school systems throughout the nation. Statewide reading scores are now watched with box-office attention, while homework has become a cause rather than a matter of practical learning. High-school principals and college presidents vie with each other in describing the direct ways in which they are forwarding our economic war against the powers of Asia and Europe.

Thus, the anxiety-driven striving of the individual *Homo economicus* has a collective national and even international aspect that makes it even more difficult to resist. Indeed, the glorification of the eighteen-hour-a-day entrepreneur that has been typical of the Reagan years can be seen as one of those American "crusades" (remember Lyndon Johnson's War on Poverty?) in which ferocious individual strivings are supposedly harmonized in the service of a larger all-American quest.

As we try to define a framework for personal happiness in which limitations are not experienced as constrictions, "having more time to oneself" is only one of the goals to be achieved. It is also possible that truly effective and productive work cannot be performed, in many cases, under the all-out workaholic banner. Hard work, in other words, may need to be accompanied by a reflective and self-evaluative frame of mind that in turn requires a periodic diminution of stress. All of us have encountered fellow workers who, when they spend less time on the job, are actually benefiting the company. We ourselves may be in that category each time we find that we are working ourselves into a frazzle. One of the good things about setting limits is that without limits there can be no shape or form.

In an even stronger sense, the vision of *Homo economicus* may be detrimental to actual economic accomplishment by implying that money is always the measure of value in the business world. The reverse is suggested by the experience of Japan, where the president of a privately owned company makes only four or five times as much as a blue-collar worker, and where senior executives regularly drop into the company cafeteria to stay in touch with those who program the robots on the assembly line. Within any American company there are those who "give" much more than they "get"—

just as there are those who do the reverse *and* those who only give you your precise money's worth.

If money is the only measure of value, and if no one does more than he or she gets paid for—if marketplace thinking, in short, is a true mode of organizing human behavior—we might expect to see the values of *Homo economicus* penetrate into private life as well as the business world. And indeed, it is not uncommon to hear an American parent criticize a child who fails to do well in school or in a Little League game by saying, "You let me down!" That, in turn, can be translated and expanded into "I gave you food, clothing, and shelter from the day you were born. You didn't carry out your half of the deal. I pay and pay and pay, but you don't pay me back!"

The notion that children are somehow indebted to their parents is so widespread that we simply take it for granted, like the air we breathe. Much more insidiously, the fiscal metaphor can invade the relations between men and women. Here are the reflections of one man, now in his mid-fifties, as he looks back on two marriages and numerous less formal contacts with those of the opposite sex:

> I really do find that I can never get over my amazement at the difference between the start and the end of a relationship. At the beginning you just can't do enough for the other person. Making them happy, putting a smile on their faces . . . that seems like the whole purpose of life. When they hurt your feelings, or you hurt theirs, making it okay again is what's on your minds.
>
> Much later, as the relationship is winding drearily down to its close, you're at the opposite end of the spectrum. The other person can't, under any circumstances, do something *right*. Joy, pleasure, contentment, togetherness have all flown out the window, never to return.

What now rules the roost is the principle of unrelenting *grudge*. They did X, Y, or Z to you. You did 1, 2, or 3 to them. Or to put it another way, you and they committed all these acts of subtraction against one another. You and they violated the code that you've got to give so-and-so much if you want to get so-and-so much.

It shows up very clearly, of course, in the area of sex. Who's doing what to whom in what particular quantity and with what particular quality is suddenly "in the air." Favors get handed out like pennies by Scrooge. Going out and having an affair becomes sweet revenge under those circumstances, though the enthusiasm engendered by the affair has to be explained, at least in part, by the fact that you're reexperiencing the notion of generosity that has leaked so completely out of your primary relationship.

When a relationship gets started, it's full of infantile joy. It's just like being a baby at the breast, giving and receiving joy. And when it's winding down, it's just like a parent/child relationship gone sour, with Mom and Dad reminding the kid of how much they've done for him or her, and the kid responding with a list of all the stuff the other kids have that Mom and Dad have been too cheap or hostile to buy.

Given the commercial orientation that all of us have in a society that is not about to give up the use of money, is there any way in which the monetary metaphor can be kept out of personal relationships? In our own conversations, we have found today's men and women more hopeful about the relationships between parents and children than about those between adult men and women. Here are the reflections of a woman just in the process of making the transition from middle age to the status of senior citizen:

> All these posters and bumper stickers asking, "Did you hug your child today?"—even when they generate parodies like "Did you hug your mailman today?"—seem to me to communicate more of a spirit of giving than you could have gotten from all of the child-rearing books of 1935 piled together. I see something going on between today's mother and child that could make a long-term difference to the way we think and behave. Most of all, today's child is more often a *wanted* child rather than an accident. Those who do get born stand a chance of receiving the right kind of attention.

Where the relationships between men and women are concerned, we found greater pessimism. The reemergence of prenuptial contracts, for example, was often cited to us as a kind of return to the Middle Ages, when marriage was seen as an economic, rather than a romantic, act. At the same time, those we interviewed conceded freely that today's prenuptial agreement is a cushion against the consequences of love not lasting, not a negation of love as such. In the words of one executive contemplating divorce:

> You probably have to see money as this very complicated emotional language. It's a way of saying things to people you love or hate. You give it to your child and you're saying—or trying to say—"I love you." You keep it from your enemy, who may need it quite badly, and it's obvious what you're saying when you do *that*. In a separation-and-divorce situation, you're communicating the full extent of your disappointment. "You couldn't give me lasting love" is what gets

communicated—"but you sure as hell are going to give me *cash!*"

Perhaps the most that men and women can hope to accomplish in today's world is to develop enough of a therapeutic viewpoint so that they can spot the money metaphor when it begins to exercise a shaping effect on their behavior toward each other. The moment when a man or woman stops to say, "I'm talking cash-register language, aren't I?" is the moment when a relationship may begin to stand a chance of surviving.

Recovering a sense of enthusiasm and generosity may require that the self be seen as more than the money it earns and more than a mere sum of the activities in which it takes part. The question is whether such a restoration of the sense of self is possible after so many years in which *talk* about the self and its development has led to some real exhaustion with the subject. To put the matter another way, isn't the rise of the vision of *Homo economicus* itself a sign of the weariness that our culture feels about intangible values and mere feelings?

The sense that "you only get what you pay for" and that no one in his right mind gives more than value for money can still be seen as quite beneficent, however, when compared with some of the narcissistic and exploitative attitudes released by a period in which "poverty sucks." To flaunt one's advantages, to show off, to boast of one's high status, to demonstrate one's superiority, to take pleasure in the envy of others—these are impulses that are once again explicitly encouraged within our culture. The ideal is once again that of the Beautiful People for whom money is no problem and life an endless fascination, whose careers (at least according to myth) never suffer a setback, and whose every word and action has a mystic significance commemorated in newspapers and magazines.

For those who cannot make it into the narrow ranks

of success, our contemporary myth offers only one alternative: Eat your heart out. Ruthless glee, in short, is again a respectable emotion.

If the renewal of the sense of personal generosity is one solution to the problem posed by *Homo economicus*—an anti-Calvinism based on the assumption that God is *not* out to get you—then the other half of the response may be the reassertion of the sense of personal value. If you don't put a strong positive evaluation on your own self and your own being, don't expect others to do it for you. But for many of us, raised from infancy in ways that imply the financial and therefore transactional metaphor, the development of a strong sense of self will not be an easy task. Women are always amazed to rediscover the extent to which they were taught that charm is the major asset they can exchange for other goods. Men, when they are thrown off some macho team or out of some macho club (often the company for which they work) are equally stunned to find that beneath all the muscle-flexing and tough talk there lies the secret terror of helplessness and impotence.

In a collective way all of the current trumpeting of external values and glamorous success may itself be a panic compensation for a world in which genuine economic progress has become very difficult to achieve. As is well known by now, the realities of inflation since 1970 have negated most apparent rises in salary. It is *only* the two-earner family that enables expenditures to continue at their present rate—and the two-earner family is by definition very vulnerable to death, disablement, unemployment, or divorce. Single women with children represent a new poverty class in our country. A tight and expensive housing market is sending neatly dressed Yuppies into SROs in some of our major cities, and whole families into the category of "the homeless" once occupied by bums and bag ladies.

A world that has become, in a number of ways, more

dangerous and desperate is one in which inner resources need to be firmed up and external dependencies—especially when they take a mainly emotional form—minimized. We live at a time when a strong sense of self may be more valuable than even money in the bank.

Part Four

I beheld the wretch—the miserable monster whom I had created.
—Mary Wollstonecraft Shelley

Whoever is capable of giving is himself rich.

—Erich Fromm

Overcoming Community Indigence

In an age when the typical employee devotes fifty to sixty hours a week to a demanding occupation, another ten hours commuting to and from the job, and between five and ten hours on the professional education and personal reading necessary to keep abreast of colleagues in the field, the limited amounts of time and energy left over from these pursuits must be hoarded carefully. Child-rearing and other domestic responsibilities consume the bulk of evenings and weekends, but there is still more for even voluntary workaholics to accommodate. In today's image-conscious society, health and fitness routines must be slotted in, along with periodic visits to hair stylist, dentist, and physician. Bills must be paid, finances managed, the needs of elderly relatives met.

At times the list seems endless, and for many Americans during the early 1980s, community service work dropped to the bottom of it. Where volunteer service to one's community was once an integral part of daily life, the new work ethic gave poignant meaning to the adage,

"Charity begins at home." After all, working as a hospital volunteer had little significance if one's own elderly and/or incapacitated parents remained unattended as a result. Donating time as a youth counselor could be nothing short of hypocritical if one's own children had no opportunity to spend time with Mom and Dad. Too, the time/energy commitment necessary for meaningful participation in even grass-roots political organizations was unthinkable when one barely had time to become conversant enough with issues and candidates to vote reasonably intelligently.

In direct corollation to the increasing number of Americans who entered or returned to the workplace in the late 1970s, the number of volunteers who were active in local communities decreased. At the end of the decade, the dramatic influx of women into the work force proved to be devastating. Traditionally, it was the stay-at-home wives and mothers who were the lifeblood of community endeavor. Without them, the social and cultural services once so abundant in the smallest hamlet—the church auxiliaries and home visitation programs, the library boards and fundraising committees, the candidates' coffees, Cub Scout dens, and bloodmobiles—over which these women had so capably and devotedly once presided inevitably dwindled.

"Women going back into the workplace has had an effect on voluntarism that's been really evident since about 1973 on," says Deborah Walsh, executive director of the Voluntary Action Center in Hartford, Connecticut,

> but I think the crisis came along in about 1978. Now, I'm not an economist, but there were a lot of reasons why women had to go back to work or begin work, and during that period, 1973 to 1978, things did change drastically. When I came to VAC in 1979, I found that the pool of women who were our mainstay in this organization was drop-

> ping off and that our agencies were crying for help: "We're just desperate to maintain these programs, but the people we used to count on during the day have evaporated, and what are we going to do?"

The negative effect on social programs of the volunteer shortage to which Walsh alludes was compounded in 1981 and 1982 by the slashing of federal funds to social service agencies. Drastic budget cuts meant that the already beleaguered organizations no longer had the option of reallocating financial resources to hire the most urgently needed help. Thus, thousands of not-for-profit organizations found themselves between a financial rock and a personnel hard place while the demand for their services mounted steadily.

"As a volunteer in the early 1960s, one could find only a handful of large, well-established agencies—churches, schools, hospitals, the Red Cross, YM and YW, Girl and Boy Scouts," recalls Denise W. Clarke, director of volunteer services at Hartford Hospital. "Today there are over 420 nonprofit agencies in the Hartford area alone seeking volunteers."

With so many women working, Clarke points out, it often fell to the elderly retired among the general population to take up the slack.

> "In the 1950s and 1960s, we still had the traditional picture of volunteering. The majority of hands-on work was done by white suburban housewives following in the tradition of their mothers and possibly grandmothers, to work for the betterment of their community—an implied obligation that went with the housewives' leisure time. When I started as a volunteer at Hartford Hospital in 1959, all the volunteers were women. Well over 90 percent were suburban housewives. All were white and represented all ages, but the

> average age was in the mid-fifties. Today, 20 to 25 percent of our adult volunteers are men, and the average age is in the late sixties. A tremendous number of retirees are showing up in volunteering in the community today.

Despite the influx of retirees, Clarke notes, the need for volunteers continued to grow. "With cost constraints in the hospital industry nationally, each year brings more requests for volunteer services from departments within the hospital—an increasingly difficult task to accomplish. It's impossible to satisfy all these requests."

Confronted with impending disaster, volunteer administrators scrambled to keep their programs afloat despite diminished resources, sometimes pressuring what few volunteers remained available to take on more and more responsibilities. The result was yet another crisis: volunteer burnout. Those who managed to carve out a few hours a week to devote to a carefully selected charity often retreated in confusion and indignation when repeatedly pressed to do more.

"I really felt proud of myself when I made the time in my hectic schedule to serve as a Cub Scout den leader," reports Cynthia, the mother of two school-age children who has always done her own housework, child care, and yard maintenance in addition to meeting the demands of her job as a freelance publications manager.

> It was a considerable sacrifice for me to do it, but I've always felt that volunteer work was very important, and I wanted to set a good example for my son and daughter. But as it turned out, whatever I did was never enough!

Together with a neighbor, Cynthia conducted weekly meetings for eight Cub Scouts at her suburban home—a complicated undertaking that involved providing refreshments, overseeing appropriate badge activities, buying supplies, keeping records, collecting dues, and transporting the boys on frequent field trips.

> If that wasn't enough, the town pack leader then asked us to take in another four boys from a den that had been disbanded for lack of volunteer leadership. Next, the metropolitan council started badgering my husband, Harry, who scarcely has time to breathe as it is, to become a council leader, which meant attending lengthy meetings on Sunday evenings and supervising monthly pack meetings and camp-outs. Without him, they said, they couldn't qualify as an official pack.

Reluctantly, Harry agreed to do what he could. "Just as soon as he attended his first meeting, he found out that no good deed goes unpunished," Cynthia recalls.

> One of the Cub Scout pack leaders, who happens to be a member of our church, started putting the pressure on Harry to get involved in one church-sponsored activity after another. Soon he was recruited to serve as a church trustee, which meant more meetings. Next, he was spending his weekends refurbishing the parish house. It just got worse and worse. I was sorry I'd ever volunteered in the first place! Before, when I just said no to everything because of my job, I was left pretty much alone. Now, both Harry and I are so frantic to meet all our job and volunteer responsibilities, we hardly ever see our own kids, let alone each other. You give a volunteer agency an inch these days, and they want to take over your life!

Cynthia's response to the increasing pressure was not unusual, nor were the extraordinary demands made upon her and her husband. The volunteers of the early 1980s were typically asked to perform the work of two or three volunteers of the 1960s. Even so, they were unable to close the gap between needed and available services, which resulted ultimately in pockets of social and cultural poverty we have termed "community indigence."

By 1983 it had become evident that it was not only the receivers of agency services who were suffering from community indigence. Those who could no longer provide those services as volunteers, primarily because of the demands of their jobs, were suffering as well. Gone was the bond of voluntarism they once shared with friends and neighbors, and with it, their strong sense of community connection. And always, there was the guilt.

"I spent up to twenty hours a week as a Little League coach for more than twelve years," says Kurt, an insurance salesman,

> but when I was promoted to regional manager, I had no choice but to give it up. Managers with my company are expected to cover a 600-square-mile territory every two weeks, and there was just no way I could handle coaching anymore. I don't mind telling you, it just about broke my heart.

Having worked with an entire generation of local youth, watching them grow into adulthood and helping them to develop physically and emotionally as committed team members, Kurt knew the importance of the work he was doing with his community's children. "It's not something that everyone enjoys doing, but I just loved it," he recalls wistfully.

> I looked forward to getting out there in the fresh air and running around with those kids, watching them come together as a cohesive

> group, cheering them on when they won and cheering them up when they lost. To them, I was "the Coach," and more than a few of them came to me with their personal problems. I was always glad to help, because I liked every one of my players. They knew it and worked their hearts out for me. They were all good kids, and I hated like hell to walk away from them.

Kurt's absence left a significant hole in the coaching schedule, and the members of his team were scattered into the remaining teams in the league, a situation that proved unsatisfactory all the way around. Several of the players, feeling abandoned and alienated, dropped out. Kurt, hearing of this, became despondent.

> I can't tell you how guilty I felt. Intellectually, I knew it wasn't my fault, and yet emotionally I suffered. In their eyes, I had sacrificed the needs of those kids to my career. But what was I supposed to do, refuse the promotion? Actually, I was tempted to do just that, but in today's job market, you don't say no to a good employer that way. The job has to come first, especially since I have two kids of my own to put through college.

The emotional conflict Kurt experienced was one familiar to hundreds of thousands of former volunteers across the country who abandoned their charitable work in favor of paid employment during the late 1970s and early 1980s. Guilt was certainly a major factor in their inner turmoil, but there was much more to it than that. Voluntarism is not, after all, a one-way street. It is an intense interaction between giver and receiver that is widely acknowledged to benefit both in innumerable ways.

"A very large part of America's attractive voluntary spirit stems from our religious heritage," states author Brian O'Connell in *America's Voluntary Spirit.*

> The lessons are as varied as the religions of the hundreds of groups that came and still come to our shores. The common root of these varied testaments is an awareness that service beyond self is both an obligation and a joy. It is the ultimate universal truth.

Even a cursory review of theological references supports this assertion. In the Bible alone, both the Old and New Testaments are liberally sprinkled with observations on the rewards of giving, for the donor as well as the donee—like this one from II Corinthians 9: 6–7.

> The point is this: he who sows sparingly will also reap sparingly, and he who sows bountifully will also reap bountifully. Each one must do as he has made up his mind, not reluctantly or under compulsion, for God loves a cheerful giver.

Earlier still, the older Eastern sects preached similarly. In Hinduism, for example, we find repeated references to the benefits of sacrifice, charity, and almsgiving, including: "Expend in alms in God's way and the rest cast by your own hands into perdition; but do good, for God loves those who do good." And, "The more that he expends for others, the more does he possess of his own; the more that he gives to others, the more does he have himself."

As, in fact, the founders of every religious sect in recorded history have known for eons, the willingness to give of oneself and of one's goods to those less fortunate does far more than meet the practical needs of those in distress. It is the very bedrock of civilized society, the basis of humane thought and activity that separates humankind from the beasts. On a purely economic plane, voluntarism is also the basis of society's primary system for the provision of goods and services.

"In our society, there are two major systems for providing goods and services," notes Vern Lake, chief of volunteer services in Minnesota's Department of Public Welfare.

> One is paid, the other voluntary. What is not done by the first is left presumptuously for the latter. It is enlightening and stimulating to note that of these two systems, the voluntary system is the major one. Paid labor is a minority increment when a full accounting for life's goods and services is made. . . . The real truth is that most of the world's work is done by volunteer labor and always has been, if the definition of voluntarism is work done without personal financial gain.

On the domestic front, Lake points out, housekeeping, nursing, child rearing, food, and laundry services are, for the most part, unpaid yet critical human services. One can add to the list lawn mowing, gardening, snow removal, building repair, other property maintenance, and errand running—all things that are customarily and routinely done "voluntarily."

At the community level, volunteers solicit money for vast numbers of charitable causes as well as contribute the money, staff political campaign offices and supply the campaign funds, join service clubs and administrate those clubs, coach youth sports, staff schools and hospitals, serve as Big Brothers and Sisters.

From a global perspective, in times of emergency it is volunteers who put out the world's fires, defend its citizens against attack, and evacuate those threatened by natural disasters. Volunteers bring the food and blankets to the hungry and cold, arrive earliest, and leave latest in every crisis. Lake concludes,

> Truth is falsified when we say the world runs on money, it runs on voluntarism. . . . Inevitably, every person becomes a volunteer. It is as impossible to run out of volunteers as it is to run out of people. And because every person becomes a volunteer but not every person goes on a payroll, voluntarism represents the largest piece in the world of work.

Lake's views on the magnitude of volunteer activities and their importance to every society are shared by many other notables. Writing in the September 1975 issue of *Redbook*, the late anthropologist Dr. Margaret Mead addressed the question Do we really need volunteers? She responded with a resounding Yes!

The people who involve themselves with unpaid public causes and charitable work of all kinds admittedly open themselves to frustration, hectic schedules, and a certain amount of drudgery. But they also open themselves to one of life's most rewarding experiences. Despite all its complications and entanglements, there is something uniquely fulfilling about *volunteering* to do something that clearly makes a difference in another person's life. It is also quite wonderful to be among other people who are voluntarily giving something of themselves to others. "When any of us take inventory of the meaning of our lives," reflects Brian O'Connell, "these special experiences have to be among the high points. Happiness is, in the end, a simple thing. Despite how complicated we try to make it or the entrapments we substitute for it, happiness is really caring and being able to do something about the caring."

In the last few years, we have witnessed a return to popularity of these age-old truths among the millions who previously walked away from their community service work in favor of paid occupations. After fifteen to twenty years of searching for total self-fulfillment in jobs that more often than not failed to live up to their expectations, Americans are rediscovering the satisfactions of volunteer work—which is why the community indigence that threatened to engulf us as recently as 1982 is now successfully being held at bay.

"I think it's true that people get a lot of psychological satisfaction that is lacking on the job through volunteer activity," confirms Deborah Walsh of Hartford's Voluntary Action Center.

> I think there's no question that you can become a very big fish in a small pond as a volunteer, whereas at work you're often anything *but*. You're a very little fish in a big pond. When a volunteer finds the right thing, it's like a different world. There's a feeling of importance, being able actually to see the difference you've made by being there. There are recognition awards; there are pins; there are banquets. And when you walk in, someone probably says, "Oh, thank God you're here!" Now, how many times do you walk into the office and have somebody say, "Thank God you're here!"? You're lucky if they don't start screaming at you about something the minute you walk in the door. So you do get a lot of good, positive stuff for yourself as a volunteer.
>
> "There are also built-in kinds of strokes, like being a Big Brother. What could be more exciting than watching a young person's life turn around? You may spend ten years at it, but you can see it. And nobody has to tell you how wonderful you are because the kid is telling you that all the time—when he calls you first when there's a crisis.

Another fringe benefit of unpaid community work is the ability to use voluntarism to explore new job possibilities, Walsh continues. "We sell it to youngsters all the time. You really want to learn about the career you think you want to go into when you graduate from high school or college? We'll put you in there doing it as a volunteer, and you can gain some work experience and put it on your resume."

The practical benefits and psychological rewards of voluntarism have combined to renew the ranks of volunteers that had shrunk so alarmingly only a few years ago. Too, volunteer administrators and their agencies have taken innovative steps to reattract their lost members, sometimes restructuring whole programs to accommodate the changed lifestyles of today's working adults. This began as early as 1981, Walsh explains.

> I was fortunate in that I had a board of directors that had vision. They had foreseen in 1978–79 that we had to do something about the issue [of fewer volunteers] if we weren't going to become extinct ourselves. The decision was made not to accept this situation but to try and look at the problem as a reality and see what we could do about it.
>
> Between 1979 and 1981 we developed a number of programs designed to attack that problem. The whole focus became one of looking at women who worked full-time and part-time—and it was really women, though it's grown now to include everybody—and saying, "These are still our volunteers. They're still people who have had a long-time commitment to helping in the community, and just because they're working full-time now doesn't necessarily mean that they'll stop." What they have to do is do it differently, and what we have to change is not the women or society but the agencies who receive the help. They are the ones who are going to have to look at themselves and think, "How can we receive the help

> we need within the given situation? How can we change what we require out of a volunteer to take advantage of their continued willingness to be of service to us?"

As it turned out, Walsh's agency, the Voluntary Action Center for the Capitol Region, Inc., pioneered a new way of attacking the volunteer shortage problem.

> The program that really stands out is the Skillsbank, a way of looking at people by skill rather than as a whole body. Instead of saying, "Here's Mr. or Mrs. Wonderful who'll do everything I need done at my agency or my hospital or whatever four days a week between nine and five," we're realizing we can't do that anymore, but we do still have pieces of them that we can use on a one-shot, short-term, release-time, or any other kind of basis. We invite these people who have limited time to become a part of this pool of volunteers, which agencies can access. We work with 410 different not-for-profit agencies in twenty-nine towns, and it hasn't taken us very long to bring them around to this way of working. In fact, the program was so excitingly successful that you'll find versions of the Skillsbank at practically every established VAC in the nation.

In such innovative ways, America's communities are replenishing their essential volunteer services. And even workaholics are gratefully acknowledging that they no longer have to choose which they will do—paid work or volunteer work. New programs and ways of structuring limited volunteer time and energy have created almost unlimited options within the arena of charitable endeavor.

"The choice as to whether or not to volunteer is not a choice between working for pay or working for free," asserts Susan Ellis, president of Energize Associates, a

Philadelphia-based national training and consulting firm specializing in voluntarism.

> Every study and poll made in the last twenty years proves that the majority of people who volunteer are indeed employed in paying jobs and therefore volunteer in addition to other responsibilities. Men have managed to be coaches, trustees, and firefighters at the same time as they have been bankers, steelworkers, and accountants. So women entering or returning to the work force are not lost to volunteering, but they are perhaps no longer available from nine to five, Monday to Friday.

The implication of all this, Ellis maintains, is that agencies need to reevaluate the way they operate. More volunteers, both male and female, might be attracted to support an organization if there are assignments open during evening or weekend hours. After all, she points out, human needs are not suspended when an agency closes, and it might even be more effective to assist clients at times that are more convenient to *them,* since most of them are also employed full-time.

"The fact is," she reflects,

> that agencies and organizations have grown complacent over the years in their recruitment of volunteers. Groups that have relied on homemakers as their main source of volunteers are faced with adaptation or dissolution. Groups that diversified their volunteer base long ago, however, are less anxious now about where their pool of volunteers will come from.

The YWCA—one of the oldest social service agencies in the country—was one organization whose volunteer force consisted for more than a century of homemakers.

The changing priorities of these women in the late 1970s set off coast-to-coast tremors that threatened to topple its traditional structure. Thoughtful consideration of how best to deal with this alarming state of affairs was what ultimately revitalized the institution.

Joyce Yarrow, executive director of the Hartford Region YWCA, recalls her agency's struggle during that period.

> Most of the volunteers who are now a part of the YWCA are working either full-time or part-time outside the home. There are very few left that are working solely within the home, and that did suggest that we had to change our way of work. We used to have volunteers take on assignments like rewriting the personnel policies, for example, and they would do the bulk of that work outside, at home, then work with staff during the day for three to four hours at a time, then come into a committee meeting to make a presentation. Now we're lucky if we can find an hour and a half of a volunteer's time when we can meet with him or her. Staff predominantly draft the policy, recommendation, or whatever; and volunteers at the meeting add, delete, and change what's presented. It's just a very different way of work.
>
> We now have more advisory volunteers as opposed to full-day working volunteers. Women come in—and men, too, for that matter—and sit in on our committees, and the bulk of the work that they do for us is at that hour-and-a-half committee meeting. Sometimes our meetings are not during the working day but in the early morning, late afternoon, or evening. What we try to do is accommodate that particular group of people who are called together on that committee or advisory group and have the meetings when

> they can attend them. It used to be that the finance committee met always on Wednesday at noontime, but that isn't necessarily the case now. That's a change from our style of work before.

Such agency efforts to restructure obsolete methods of operation have gone far toward alleviating the problem of community indigence. Other promising efforts have stemmed from federal encouragement to private industry to become involved in community service programs. "It started with the Reagan Administration," says Deborah Walsh, pointing out that this was the same administration that curtailed social program funds in the early 1980s.

> He started the whole thing by telling big business that with governmental cutbacks they were going to have to assume some of the responsibility. Reagan put a very high priority on volunteers. He gave these wonderful speeches in the early 1980s saying that volunteers are the backbone of America, that we can't rely on government money any more, and so forth. The corporations perceived this as a lessening of the demands on their pocketbooks. They felt that they no longer had to give big money. I mean, they gave the same dollars as before, but at the same time we helped them to get their employees involved in the community.

What volunteer agencies did in 1981, 1982, and 1983, Walsh says, was to convince the corporations that an important part of corporate social responsibility was the support of employee voluntarism.

> We did enormous numbers of things in line with that effort, ending up with a full-time person in this agency, called our corporate liaison. His

> job is to work with corporations of any size, on request, to develop volunteer programs . . . and they come to us in incredible numbers. We can sell this so easily because the fact is (and they genuinely believe this, and so do we) that a corporation whose employees get involved in the community has a better chance of retaining its top-level employees.
>
> The New England industrial cities suffer from an excess of weather, commuter traffic, and air pollution. If you are a top-level executive, you can make choices about where you prefer to locate. As we can't control weather, pollution, and traffic, we have to develop the physical, educational, and cultural environment that retains these people so they do not go elsewhere. And very definitely, if you contribute both cash to the arts and the talents of your top executives to develop quality programming and keeping things floating at the Hartford Ballet, you'll be helping to make Hartford a sexy place to stay.

Regarding the effect of the new American work ethic, Walsh agrees that we are seeing a return to the values of community and to the rewards of volunteer service that have been missing from the lives of those who embraced the work-is-everything philosophy in recent decades.

> I think that people are looking for ways out of the tedium of their jobs. Women who were forced back into the workplace in the 1970s, in particular, haven't let go yet of the way things were when they had the freedom to spend the time with their families that they wished, or if they wished.
>
> In terms of individual involvement, our sense is that there are always two parts to a person's

> involvement. One is the altruistic side, which is bolstered by a little bit of guilt at having to leave the library board or whatever they were doing before they went back to work. So employees have been really glad to have the corporations sanction that, saying it's okay, go ahead and do that. Another part of it is purely selfish, and I love it, because I think that if those of us who work full-time and have families and do everything under the sun aren't selfish about why we're going outside of our workplace, we're making a serious mistake. I think a lot of people are rebelling against the work-is-everything ethic. They're looking at their work as something they have to do that's tedious and time-consuming and intense, and they need an outlet. You can go to a gym and do workouts, or you can go out and do something as a volunteer that's totally unrelated to job activities.

Gradually, then, Americans are rediscovering the soul-renewing properties of voluntarism and are recognizing its possibilities for self-definition, unavailable from many paid occupations. Defining oneself solely in terms of what one does to earn a paycheck has turned out to be the path to a one-dimensional existence, and in much the same way that they are giving renewed time and attention to the cultivation of personal relationships, workers are now actively seeking via community service the things that make life worth living. No longer the exclusive province of stay-at-home wives and mothers, voluntarism is opening new doors for Americans of both sexes, every age group, and every ethnic derivation.

"Many years ago volunteers were generally either teenagers prodded by their mothers to be hospital 'pinkies' or club women who were anxious to do their bit to help those less fortunate," recalls Peggy Servick, director of volunteer services at Saint Francis Hospital and Medical Center.

> How the picture has changed! No longer can one draw a prototype of the typical volunteer. They may be suffering from an emotional problem and trying to reenter the world of work. They may be in doubt about what career to follow. Volunteering can be an excellent tool for making a career decision. They may be in their seventies or eighties and want to get out and meet people. They may have boring full-time jobs and need an outlet. They may have to do community work as part of a school project. They may also be mended cancer or heart patients or multiple sclerosis victims wanting to be support volunteers in one of those areas.

Denise Clarke of Hartford Hospital concurs:

> I have seen young adults turned-on to volunteering, gaining a realization that volunteering can be self-satisfying and fulfilling. They will be back to work many more hours when they retire because their first attempt has been a positive one.
>
> I and my counterparts are also interviewing more and more young adults who are looking for satisfaction through volunteering and weekly relief from a dull, tedious job working with machines, statistics, or data processing, especially. Many are looking at volunteering as career exploration to research job changes to human-focused fields such as health care. Volunteering can satisfy many motivational needs.
>
> Once a volunteer, always a volunteer. The act brings a gratification one cannot obtain in

> paid employment or self-centered, self-seeking leisure pursuits.

Though the number and variety of people seeking volunteer assignments in the last two years is certainly encouraging, it can also be bewildering to even experienced program administrators; but most have become expert at matching a volunteer's assignment criteria to an agency's—or even an individual recipient's—needs. Deborah Walsh recalls a particularly serendipitous match she made:

> About three years ago I got a call from a man who was blind. He said, "I really need someone to read my mail. I'm being taken." And I said, well, you contact thus and so agency and they'll do this and that, and he said, "No, they won't. I've been a member of those organizations for years, and they just don't have readers. What can I do?" I said, well, unfortunately, not much, but let me think about it. Then a week or so later somebody called from a nonprofit band. This band consists of members who are all in their seventies and eighties. They do gigs, playing in nursing homes, everywhere. They were looking for a piano player, and from my earlier conversation, I happened to know that this blind man played the piano—and very well. So I thought, Aha! I've got it—a trade! So I said, "If you can find somebody to read this man's mail, I'll get him to play the piano for you." He's been playing ever since, and he's wonderful!

Such minor miracles are what keeps a volunteer administrator going, Walsh says, but within the last two years the overall situation has also shown heartening signs of improvement. Internal program changes made by volunteer agencies have made a significant difference in their ability to attract volunteers with limited amounts of time and energy, and the simultaneous turnaround in corporate attitudes has made it possible for even line employees to get involved in community work via release time. "The basic message is that voluntarism is alive and well in America," she exults. "We're talking about 60 percent of all adults who do something, according to terms defined in a 1981 Gallup Poll. That's an incredible number, considering all the other things people have to do today."

This isn't to say that communities are surfeited with volunteers, even so. The experts agree that despite the rededicated efforts of agencies, individuals and the business community, the demand for volunteer services still outstrips the supply in many program areas. While the number of volunteers generally has grown, the number of *traditional* volunteers—those able to be personally present during daytime hours—has decreased drastically, and there are many programs, such as the Boy and Girl Scouts, Camp Fire Girls, and other youth programs, that simply cannot function without these people to call upon during regular business hours.

"The pool of volunteer candidates is expanding," explains Peggy Servick,

> but keeping pace with—and perhaps moving ahead of—that expansion are the multiple agencies seeking volunteers. The pie may be bigger, but each slice is smaller. More and more agencies are seeking volunteers. Listen to the radio, and you'll hear a stream of public service announcements for this organization or that, each promising to fill the need of a particular volunteer.

Such expectations are, of course, unrealistic. Still, we are slowly coming to realize that while "what we do" may indeed be "who we are," we are capable of doing a far greater number of diverse and rewarding tasks, both paid and unpaid, than we have chosen to do in the recent past. We are realigning our priorities, separating our identities just a bit from our paid occupations, and searching out a wider spectrum of activities to meet our complex needs as total human beings.

Joyce Yarrow of the YWCA comments on this trend.

> If you're really committed to what you're doing, it can be all-consuming. The word *workaholic* is a very real word. You can say "voluntary" workaholic, but I think very often you don't realize that you've volunteered to become that. When it becomes overwhelming, sometimes we blame the job—the work is too hard, or the corporation or the organization is too demanding upon us and they don't respect who we are or value us. But I think we own some of that ourselves, and we have to find ways of taking control of our own time, our work, what we're going to give, and how we're going to give it. We have to find where we want that self-fulfillment.
>
> There's a work life, but it isn't necessarily everything in the whole wide world. The workplace seldom gives the recognition and appreciation we all need. If you lose your job, you don't lose your life, but I have seen too many people who felt that if they've lost their job, that's the end of the world. If you can find who you are and what gives you personal reward and fulfillment, you might get that from your job and feel great satisfaction. But you can also find ways to get it in other areas of your life.

It takes a little bit of doing, Yarrow admits, but it is well worth the effort. She herself went through the process some four or five years ago, emerging with a new balance of work and personal interests.

> I work just as hard as I always did, but I work smarter—more effectively and efficiently, and I have far more reward from my work life as well as from my personal life. If you can feel successful as a *person,* it's much more than your work life. It's also your church life and your home life and serving in other organizations, plus leisure time activities. These all can complement who you are and how *you* feel successful.

There is no doubt that we are doing things differently today than we were twenty years ago, or that economic and societal pressures have driven us to expend more time and energy than in previous years on our jobs. But as we strive to put work in its place, we are simultaneously redefining the concept of "work" itself, recognizing that unpaid labor—the work we do for love instead of money, if you will—may well be a truer measure of our inner selves than our paid occupations. When we choose a charitable undertaking (and one of the great pleasures of voluntarism is the ability to choose what we will do, not acquiesce to someone else's notion of what we must do), we are expressing ourselves as individuals in ways we can never hope to do on the job. As volunteers, we are uniquely ourselves.

"Since ancient times, there always has been a point of view that believes mandatory public service should be required in any society," comments George Moody, president, chief operating officer, and a director of Security Pacific National Bank.

> I don't agree with that. I believe that much of the personal satisfaction that comes from volunteering is the knowledge that those who choose to volunteer are serving beyond the required, serving above the mandatory. Voluntarism is a personal statement of involvement and commit-

> ment that cannot be duplicated through mandatory quotas or involuntary conscription.

Perhaps in the months and years ahead, a greater number of American workaholics will relearn this basic truth.

The trouble with the rat race is that even if you win, you're still a rat.

—Lily Tomlin

OPTING OUT

Since the early 1960s Americans have been actively engaged in the pursuit of options—the creation of a larger menu of life choices from which to select. "Personal choices remained rather narrow and limited from the postwar period through much of the 1960s," says social commentator John Naisbitt in *Megatrends*.

> Many of us lived the simple lives portrayed in such television series as *Leave It to Beaver* and *Father Knows Best:* Father went to work, Mother kept house and raised 2.4 children. There were few decisions to make; it was an either/or world.

Such is clearly not the case today. The unprecedented social upheavals of the late 1960s and 1970s, which planted the seeds of rebellion in the hearts of those long discontented with traditional roles assigned to them, presaged the era of incredible diversity which is the 1980s. "The either/or choices in the basic areas of family and work have exploded into a multitude of highly individual arrangements and lifestyles," Naisbitt concludes.

Women, of course, have long known that an increased number of options is what liberation is all about. Yet despite the rich and varied options now available to men and women both, for the most part they have declined to take advantage of them. Until the present moment, in fact, Americans have simply exchanged one set of shackles (the stereotypical roles of breadwinner and housewife) for another (slavish devotion to the notion of career success).

In recent months, however, a generalized awareness of this trend has begun to surface. The Baby Boomers, who so fervently embraced the new American work ethic some ten to twenty years ago, have started to acknowledge the narrowness of the path they have chosen. After years and years of nonstop workaholism, the Boomers are beginning to rethink their earlier choices, to recognize the wealth of diversity around them, and to remember that the point of having options is to exercise them now and again. For many, life has become a rat race, and the more courageous among us are opting out.

Consider these early signs of backlash: The corporate executive of two decades ago accepted the fact that periodic relocation was a part of the job; today's executives, who very likely have working spouses, are far more resistant to relocation, especially if employers fail to help spouses find new work after moving.

It used to be that working meant joining a factory or an office after graduation from high school or college and working that organization's regular full-time schedule until retirement; now workers are "hiring employers" according to their own needs and preferences, selecting full-time or part-time schedules, deciding to work out of an office or their own homes, and exploring flex-time or job-sharing options.

Traditionally, there have been men's jobs and women's jobs, but with women making up nearly half of the total American work force, such gender distinctions are yielding to multiple options for both sexes. Today, male secretaries, nurses, and telephone operators scarcely rate a second glance; female bus drivers, repairpersons, or construction workers are no longer oddities. As a result, the longstanding pay disparities between traditionally male and female jobs are slowly disappearing, making a wider range of job categories equally attractive to the members of both sexes.

The two-earner trend within families has created a huge number of lifestyle options for both partners in a marriage, provided they are not incurably addicted to two steady, full-time incomes. Both men and women are beginning to acknowledge that they have choices—real choices that are theirs to make if they only will—about the ways in which they choose to work and live. Employers no longer hold all the cards.

"It is easier," says Naisbitt, "to ride a trend in the direction it is already going," which is why so many of us unquestioningly climbed onto the work-is-everything bandwagon. But the trend of total devotion to career has peaked, and more and more folks are choosing to buck it these days. Instead of buying into the new work ethic, Americans are taking advantage of today's multiple choices to create more balanced, emotionally satisfying lives for themselves and their families.

"The trouble with the rat race is that even if you win, you're still a rat," says comedienne Lily Tomlin, tersely summarizing the conclusion to which millions of her contemporaries have come after decades on the career treadmill. Since the mid-1960s we have been conditioned to think of ourselves as successful only if we progress satisfactorily within the work place. Journalist Hilary Cosell explains how women, particularly, were encouraged to believe this.

> We wouldn't succeed by displaying any traditional kinds of female behavior. Marriage was a prison; suburbia, death; and children, a lifetime of slavery. No, sir, not me. I got the message, and

> the truth set me free. I will be successful. Earn lots of money; be a professional. . . . And, of course, success meant other things, too. It meant freedom from economic and emotional dependence on men. It meant you were a special person, a brave and strong pioneer hacking your way through the jungle to beat a path for successive generations of women to follow, superior to women without success.

After living out this philosophy for a number of years, however, women—and men, too—are listening to the inner voices that question its validity. They are opting out of the rat race, recognizing the limited rewards of the career-centered way of life, and redefining success in ways that reflect the broad spectrum of their needs as human beings.

A thirty-three-year-old engineer of our acquaintance, once totally engulfed by the demands of his career, has found that his relationship with a colleague has turned to love. "She and I are making each other very happy," he reports with a smile,

> and much healthier than we were a year ago. We're taking time to enjoy life, to participate in a softball league, to window shop and talk and plan our life together. We still work hard, but we have both revised our workaholic tendencies of the last few years. We haven't abandoned our career aspirations, but we've added new goals in other areas, as well.

A woman in her mid-forties, whose husband works in a different department of the same insurance company, comments:

> After nearly fifteen years of hardly talking with each other because of the time pressures of

> our jobs, my husband and I have rediscovered each other, and it's just great. I had almost forgotten what a wonderful person Al is. Now we try to commute together and have lunch at least once a week in the company cafeteria. Al is thinking less about the next step up on the career ladder and more about taking a lateral transfer into a less demanding position. We still enjoy our jobs, but we've gotten back something that is even more important to us: our marriage.

All of these people are engaged in redefining "success" in more personal terms. Still, it appears to be the women who are leading the way. Having fought long and hard for equal opportunities for success within the workplace, they have weighed the merits of distinguished careers and found them lacking unless more personal kinds of success accompany them. "This is what I think about success now," says Cosell.

> I think that when you toss away the rhetoric and push the manifestos off the table, there are very few women who do not define success primarily in terms of their personal lives, in terms of their marital and motherhood status. I have tried *not* to do this. I have denied it. Refused to believe it. Scorned it. And ultimately I was a liar.

To test the new perceptions of her colleagues, Cosell asked a dozen female colleagues to define a successful woman. All were employed, earning at least $32,000 annually, and between the ages of twenty-six and forty. Here are some of their definitions:

- A successful woman is someone who is successful at life, not a job.
- A successful woman is a Superwoman who has a husband, child, and a good job.

- I used to think it was having a great job, money, and some power. Now my success is my daughter. The rest is just work.

It is interesting, Cosell notes, that not one respondent cited the chairmanship of GM or the attainment of high political office in her definition of success. Still, the career element was included in most replies, and this represents a distinct change from earlier decades. Something clearly has been *added* to women's successful self-definition, but the values of home and family remain as deeply rooted as ever and are resurfacing as women opt out of a one-dimensional existence in the work place.

"Many outward trappings have changed," Cosell concludes,

> but the interior landscape, the emotional lives of women, seem to have remained largely the same regarding the most basic definitions of self and success. . . . The broader definition of success I am searching for will neither consign women to the home and dependence on men nor nail them to a cross of professionalism.

The current reassessment of the validity of the modern work ethic has spawned a number of surveys and questionnaires in popular magazines. The findings of most indicate that women have been quicker overall to acknowledge the down side of careerism, but that men are beginning to realize that they, too, have been seduced by a faithless lover.

In the October 1985 issue of *Working Woman,* Julia Kagan summarized the results of a March survey to which 11,000 readers responded. The question was "What does success really mean to you?" and the responses clearly indicated that Americans are realizing that putting career success ahead of such priorities as a good family life or rewarding relationships does *not* produce success or satisfaction—for women or for men.

The priorities of the sexes do differ, with more men indicating the amassing of money as a priority and more women listing generalized "career success," whether or not accompanied by an awesome paycheck. Women and men who listed becoming financially well off as their *top* priority also said they were less satisfied with their lives and their relationships, if any, than others are. "What we can't tell, however," says Kagan, "is whether an unhappy life is a cause or an effect of a money-centered ethos. But," she continues, "these results would seem to call for a large wastebasket into which [we] can toss all those books that advise us sternly to put success first."

The greater willingness of women to abandon the notion of work-as-life and to acknowledge their need for close personal ties outside the workplace to lend balance and perspective to their lives seems to give them an edge in their redefinition of success. Their new feeling seems to be that the multiple roles, responsibilities, and options that are making modern life a very complicated affair also offer multiple opportunities for personal happiness. For example, the woman who finds that she is less than ecstatic with her career progress at any given time still seems able to take great satisfaction from her relationships with family and friends, from community work and personal pursuits. It is precisely this refusal to see themselves as single-faceted human beings that is allowing women to opt out of the new American work ethic without apology.

The woman who sees herself as successful in 1986 is likely to have multiple aspects to her life and to be consciously working toward expanding her opportunities for self-fulfillment outside the workplace as well as within it. Instead of choosing a rigid, linear path to success in a single arena, she is finding creative new ways to put together a variety of rewarding endeavors, both paid and unpaid. The formula is different for each woman, and it generally is an accurate reflection of her individual values. The new definition of success seems to be having the freedom to define all the pieces of oneself and the opportunity to fulfill them, sequentially or simultaneously. Career is definitely on the agenda for most, but when to work, at what, and for how long are up to each woman.

After a decade or more of choosing between evils—total devotion to a career at the expense of a personal life, or a manic existence in which home, family, and career were juggled frantically by an unwilling Superwoman—women are recognizing that they now have more attractive choices. "In my Superwoman era I was determined to have it all," says Sara, who has juggled domestic concerns with career demands for most of her adult life.

> But about the time I turned thirty-five, it dawned on me that having it all meant having to *do* it all. Since that's impossible, I wasn't doing anything particularly well. I had become a slave to my own idea of success and had forgotten that there were really a number of other choices open to me.

Those choices, Sara realized, included working only part-time, working not at all until her children entered school, dividing child-rearing responsibilities with her husband (who might also change the structure of his paid employment), and delegating a greater portion of her domestic responsibilities to paid help. Each choice involved some measure of sacrifice—mostly financial—but each also offered the opportunity to live a more satisfying life overall. Ultimately, Sara opted out of her technical-writing position at an electronics firm to give more time and attention to her young children. Though she was no longer bringing home a hefty corporate paycheck, she was able to secure freelance work to do at home on a part-time basis. Since day-care expenses for the children had virtually been eliminated from the budget, the difference between her previous and present earnings is scarcely noticeable, she says.

As increasing numbers of women make similar choices, they are reassured by the supportive responses of their peers, whom they at first feared would sneer at them for caving in under domestic pressures. More and more, the attitude is "Do what's best for you, not what the media tell you you ought to be doing." While the modern woman is just as committed to living the fullest possible life as her 1970s sisters were, she is taking a more thoughtful, long-term view of her future, considering the merits of having it all sequentially instead of simultaneously in an orderly progression of work- and home-focused periods that allow her to concentrate the greater part of her attention and energy in one or the other arena.

Changing careers is another way in which women are opting out of the rat race. When a second income is necessary to a family's survival, as it so often is today, it may not be possible for a woman to stop working altogether. Very often, it isn't even desirable for reasons quite apart from money. However, it may be that a job with predictable hours, more vacation and personal leave time, and benefits more suited to the woman juggling home and job responsibilities is a desirable alternative to the fast-track position selected years ago.

Confronted with the untenable prospect of twenty-four-hour-a-day Superwomanhood for the duration of their children's upbringing, women are matter-of-factly assessing their marketable skills and job interests, deciding the circumstances under which they might use them to best advantage, then selecting from the options now available to them. Self-employment is an increasingly popular choice as women discover that a host of lucrative activities, from accounting and advertising to training and travel arrangement, can be performed competently and conveniently from home-based offices. Sales, insurance investigation, word processing, telephone marketing, answering services, editing, and transcription are other job categories now heavily populated by self-employed women who have awakened to the many benefits of working primarily at home.

In a wide variety of ways, then, women are recognizing the pitfalls of the work-is-everything ethic and are turning away from it in growing numbers. A bit more slowly, but just as enthusiastically, the men in their lives are beginning to join them. Though slightly more reluctant to face up to the folly of committing themselves to a life spent primarily in the workplace, men are, at last, admitting that the multiple options of the 1980s—created by the social movements of earlier decades and by the relatively new phenomenon of having two wage earners in the family—are available to them, too.

Survey results indicate that financial success is still overwhelmingly important to most men, but what the results don't specify is that *how* wealth is accumulated has become relatively unimportant to them. It is still appealing to earn financial security via a top executive position, but it would be equally satisfying to attain it by winning the lottery, inheriting a fortune, or discovering oil in the back yard. Men's new attitude seems to be that as long as it's money, legally obtained, it will do very nicely, thank you.

It remains true that men are more reluctant than women to relinquish the community status associated with a corporate title and the accompanying paycheck. Still, new precedents are being set every day, and it's evident that the definition of success is slowly changing for men, too.

Dan, a computer programmer, tells the story of going

out to dinner with a number of male colleagues from different companies shortly after his daughter was born. The men gathered in the restaurant bar, and they spent more than an hour talking not about business but about their children and their involvement with them. When their table was finally ready, the bartender—a woman—tapped Dan on the shoulder. "I've got to tell you," she said, "that's the most unbelievable conversation I've ever heard in a group of men at this bar. No stocks, no gold prices, no football scores. I loved it!"

Although that particular incident occurred more than a year ago, Dan recognized it as the beginning of his emotional reorientation away from his job and toward his new family. Within months, he had left his position in a high-tech firm where he had worked for more than ten years and obtained a new position with the state university.

> I made the shift mainly because it was clear to me that if I stayed where I was, I would have less and less time with my daughter. Five years ago, I never would have thought that way, probably because I didn't know anyone else then who had the same feelings. But now I do. In fact, I know several guys at the university who walked away from the big bucks to spend more time with their families—and it's okay to talk about it! It's a whole new ballgame today. It used to be that only women would talk openly about untraditional approaches to problems in their lives. Now men can do it, too, and not be looked upon as oddballs.

Trying something new has become the fantasy of millions of middle-age Baby Boomers. The most stimulating occupation in the world can pall after ten or fifteen years, and it often has, leaving men to inquire of themselves, "So, what's next?" The old pattern of working for forty years for the same company has changed dramatically, with most men changing jobs and/or careers not just once but several times over the course of their work lives. The stigma once suffered by the job-changer has largely disappeared, and men are feeling freer than ever before to rethink their earlier choices, consider new options, and choose from among them. The resulting changes men are making in their lives more accurately reflect their new needs and changing priorities, and they are more willing to consider additional changes as time goes by.

Instead of locking themselves into one inflexible pattern for the duration, men are starting to make new choices about their lifestyles as a *whole,* not just about their work. In recent years many have experimented with the reversal of traditional men's and women's roles. John, a university administrator for nearly twenty years, tells about his experiences with role reversal:

> About four years ago I got very discouraged with my job. While I had enjoyed teaching in my early years at the university, administration proved to be a whole different thing. There was a lot of personnel supervision involved, and the staff were chronically unhappy because budgets were so tight and job advancement was practically nil. My days became one long, endless round of wrangling over promotions, purchases, budgets. Every morning, it was a struggle for me to get up and drag myself to work.

Meanwhile, John's wife had been rising speedily through the ranks at a major testing firm and loving every minute of it after a dozen years at home with the couple's children. Her salary was more than ample for the two to live on.

> One day, when I was doing our tax return, I said, "Why am I putting myself through this? We

> give the government half of our combined salaries anyway." So I talked it over with Angela, and we decided that I would quit my job and stay home and take care of the house and the yard and the errands and all that sort of thing. She loved the idea!

For nearly three years, now, John has taken over everything at home. To his wife's huge delight, he even learned to cook respectably—a task she had never enjoyed. "Surprisingly," John says today,

> I've enjoyed the work very much. When Angela is at work, I find I have plenty of time to do some scholarly research and writing, which satisfies my need to keep my hand in the academic world. Otherwise, I guess I'm what you'd call a househusband. But I'm also what *I'd* call a happy man!

As positive as the potential of role reversal is, the motives behind it are critical. For example, it is possible that a man may simply be yearning to free himself from corporate life so strongly that he fantasizes about the joys of domestic life, then finds the reality most unsatisfactory. Running from a negative situation into an unknown alternative can turn an already bad scene into a disaster, as more than one couple has discovered.

The unknown alternative might be a brand new, and totally inappropriate, career instead of role reversal. The television show *Newhart* has apparently prompted an unprecedented number of men to yearn for the life of a New England innkeeper, and Vermont has been inundated, a local realtor reports, with hundreds of Sunday shoppers hoping to spot the perfect property with which to begin a new way of life. "I can spot one before he even gets out of the car," says Mac, a native Vermonter and a realtor specializing in the sale of commercial properties.

> Typically, he's about 50, a little paunchy, with a wistful look on his face. He's driving a Buick or a Lincoln with New York or Massachusetts plates, and his wife trails along after him with the air of humoring somebody who's a little deranged. He's had it with the corporate rat race, he says, and he wants to live the life of the gentleman innkeeper. And he has no idea whatsoever what that really means!

Thanks to *Newhart,* Mac reveals, there is a common misconception that innkeeping is a very restful, refined occupation. Unlike the sitcom version, which has Newhart stepping out of his cozy den every now and then to exchange pleasantries with his beautiful wife and loyal staff or to enjoy a sumptuous dinner in front of a roaring fire in the dining room of his historic inn, the reality of innkeeping is decidedly earthy. Those of Mac's acquaintance customarily work a seven-day week, tending to everything from faulty plumbing, unreliable kitchen help, and demanding guests to the endless task of maintaining their property.

> The Sunday shoppers see only what they want to see . . . the fun of presiding over a brass-railed bar and serving vegetables grown out back in the garden. When it comes to handling intoxicated guests and filling in for the chef that doesn't show up at five o'clock one morning during the height of the skiing season, they don't want to know about it. But that's what innkeeping is all about, and they'd better be sure they have the whole picture before they change their way of life.

To separate the dreamers from the genuine prospects, Mac has devised a simple screening procedure. He puts interested buyers together with a young couple in the area that has been struggling to keep their inn in the black for several years now.

> Laura and Tom knew what they were getting into, and they've made it work, but they're always glad to set other folks straight. After a day or two of watching those kids clean bathrooms, change bed linen, haul ashes out of eighteen fireplaces, set tables, deal with suppliers, keep books, run dozens of errands, cover the desk, and try to keep a hundred guests happy, most prospective innkeepers just climb on back into their Buicks and head back to the city.

Still, changing careers is for men, as it is for women, one way to opt out of the trap of workaholism, and, like women, men are choosing in growing numbers to manage small businesses that offer more control over, and flexibility within, their lives as a whole. In fact, the many Baby Boomers who have already abandoned corporate careers and established their own businesses are largely responsible for the new job opportunities now open to their former peers in the corporate trenches. The Boomers who were initially left behind in big corporations are now feeling the squeeze as advancement becomes more difficult. Soon, they are likely to join their fellows on the outside, seeking in today's variety of flourishing entrepreneurial endeavors the professional challenges that increasingly elude them in the corporations in which they have spent the last fifteen to twenty years.

Others, like our programmer friend Dan, choose to remain within an organizational structure, but in a setting that permits more freedom in their personal lives. The fast track within a single corporation or other organization, with its long hours, nonexistent weekends, and endless stresses, is no longer meekly accepted by today's male executives. Such expectations on the part of employers are often met with resistance, requests for lateral transfers to other positions, or outright refusal to comply.

Even when a promotion and a significant raise are on the horizon, a growing number of men are declining to be transferred—and not just within the corporate ranks, either. Some ten years ago, for example, special agents with the Justice and Treasury Departments of the U.S. Government were instructed to expect periodic transfers over the course of their twenty-year careers and were required to sign acceptances of this policy as a prerequisite to getting their jobs. Every two or three years they were expected to uproot their wives and children and to go wherever the Federal Bureau of Investigation, the Bureau of Alcohol, Tobacco and Firearms, or the Drug Enforcement Administration, among other agencies, specified, regardless of an agent's personal preferences or family difficulties associated with relocation.

In the early days of the 1980s, however, resistance to the relocation policy surfaced. It was not uncommon for an agent confronted with a transfer order to plead hardship, request a transfer to another government agency until his retirement, or if no other choice remained, to quit outright, sacrificing his hard-earned equity in the government pension program.

When a mass relocation program was announced in 1981 to "broaden agents' experience," and hundreds of agents' names appeared on transfer lists, a class-action suit was instituted. Faced with the possibility of having to engage in a lengthy legal wrangle, to operate with severely restricted manpower in the event of a mass walkout, or to recruit and train hundreds of replacements for experienced agents, the bureaucratic powers retreated in confusion. After delays amounting to more than a year, the relocation program was totally reorganized—on a voluntary participation basis.

Such victories augur well as men join women in striving to change the *status quo* in the workplace, but they remain few and far between. For every such compromise on the employer's side of the negotiating table, there are a hundred on the employee's side, a trade-off deemed unsatisfactory by workers of both sexes today. For this reason, it is still most often necessary to change careers—or to change jobs within a general career category—to achieve more control and flexibility in one's work life.

For many, it is not so much the nature of the job as the nature of the job *site* that makes the critical difference. While some do thrive in the generally more hectic, socialized atmosphere of the corporate environment, many are eager to leave the freeway and its traffic jams behind them and work out of their homes. This option is becoming more and more viable thanks to the advent of "telecommunication," a process that has given rise to thousands of small businesses that are conducted almost entirely by computer.

Jack Nilles, a senior research associate at the University of Southern California, and the person who claims to have coined the term "telecommuter" back in 1973, estimates that there are about 20,000 telecommuters at work in America today. He predicts that the number could easily reach 10 million by 1990, with virtually all such workers operating out of home-based offices. So far, he is on target, with small software, technical editing, word processing, and research companies springing up in houses, apartments, and condos all over the country.

Because the U.S. economy is changing, moving away from heavy industry and toward the exchange of information, telecommuting is now a viable option for workers interested in a wide variety of jobs. It has been made possible by the proliferation of the microcomputer which, along with the intelligent terminal, is getting easier to use and less costly with each passing day. Another gain for telecommuting has been the creation of thousands of well-organized, easily accessed databases, allowing at-home operators to conduct all kinds of research, from geneology to patent searches, for a fee.

"With a decent micro or terminal or both," says Kathleen K. Wiegner and Ellen Paris in the September 12, 1983, issue of *Forbes*, "any moderately intelligent, curious person can retrieve data, process it on site, and send it to another computer without leaving his home—a portion (of the expenses) of which the IRS probably allows him to deduct."

The attractions of telecommuting vary from practitioner to practitioner. Some find that telecommuting offers a way to be productive, not to mention solvent, in their later years. To handicapped persons, telecommuting offers a significant range of employment opportunities that might otherwise be unavailable to them. But increasingly, telecommuters are just plain folks who enjoy the opportunity to spend less time involved in office politics and commuting, and more time interacting with their children and spouses. Advocates swear that telecommuting has even increased their productivity, allowing them to work in concentrated sessions rather than engage in social chitchat with colleagues in an office, run from one unnecessary meeting to another, have lunch with business associates, and pursue other activities extraneous to the job.

Marsha Kendrickson is one telecommuter who is finding this to be true. A former copy editor for a Los Angeles newspaper, Kendrickson left her job a year ago to have a baby. Rather than consign her infant son to day care, she decided to set up a home office with the appropriate computer technology and go into business for herself as an all-around researcher. For $45 an hour, she rents her services to clients who haven't the resources or the skills to navigate the complex waters of electronic information on their own. A small engineering firm trying to win a regentrification project, for example, may enlist her aid in obtaining demographic and cost statistics that would cost them thousands of dollars to unearth on their own.

At present, Kendrickson works approximately twenty hours a week and nets more than $3,000 each month.

> It's something I do well, and I'm well paid for doing it. But even better than that, I have the freedom to do the work when it's convenient. If it's a sunny afternoon, and I want to take Jimmy to the park, no problem. We go. The database I need for the day's project is just as accessible at 8:30 P.M., after Jimmy's in bed, as it is in the middle of the traditional work day.

Indirectly, Kendrickson's success with telecommuting has created new options for her husband, as well. When Marsha is ready to work perhaps thirty-five hours a week, he says, her income will be sufficient to allow him to return to graduate school, where he plans to finish an Ed.D. that has been languishing incomplete for three years while he pursued a fast-track career in data management. With that credential safely in hand, he will drop out of the rat race, he says, to pursue a new career in college teaching.

These, then, are some of the ways in which American workers are opting out of the one-dimensional existence created by the new work ethic. One by one, they are calling a halt to a way of life dictated by one's paid occupation, reassessing their options, and making new choices based on a broader spectrum of human needs.

As the trend of voluntary workaholism peaks and wanes, a new trend is emerging that promises to bring Americans closer to their roots as a free people than perhaps ever before. While we abandon more traditional concepts of work, we are renewing our spirit of entrepreneurism with all of its connotations of strength and optimism, innovation and individualism. We have come, as a society, full circle, returning in this technological era to the excitement and hope and pioneer spirit that is, after all, our heritage.

Part Five

The future . . . seems to me no unified dream but a mince pie, long in the baking, never quite done.

—E. B. White

An era can be said to end when its basic illusions are exhausted.

—Arthur Miller

FUTURE TRENDS

With each passing day, more and more Americans are thoughtfully reexamining the workaholic way of life to which they more or less willingly committed themselves a decade or more ago. Negative fallout is everywhere apparent: estranged spouses and children, a dearth of close personal relationships of any kind, total vulnerability to organizational politics and policies, stalled professional and personal growth. As the Baby Boomers hit mid-career bottlenecks on the path to advancement as the result of their vast numbers, the status and self-esteem once to be found within corporate ranks are steadily ebbing, and tying one's ego to the size of one's paycheck has become increasingly risky.

This is, after all, the era in which a man who can hit a baseball one out of every three times at bat earns far more than a surgeon who saves 95 percent of his or her patients' lives, in which a mediocre rock singer's earnings quickly outstrip those of the most talented classical musician, and in which anyone with a dollar to buy a lottery ticket can become a multimillionaire overnight. In such an era, salary cannot rationally be considered a reliable measure of self-worth, and so for many, working hard to achieve financial rewards has become an obsolete ethic.

Thus, if work no longer offers the allures of wealth and societal esteem, what can be its future in America—or more accurately, what is the future of America's workers?

Surprisingly bright, according to the experts and the statistics, with every indicator pointing to exciting new opportunities for a broader-based, more balanced way of life in which work will remain a significant, but no longer overwhelming, factor. Through the end of the century, several major trends are emerging, all of which have very positive implications for tomorrow's worker in terms of putting work in its place.

- America's evolution from an industrial to an information-based economy will result in continued growth in service jobs.

After a decade of dismal unemployment statistics, the U.S. civilian unemployment rate dropped to 6.9 percent in December 1985—the lowest figure in nearly six years. Continued growth in service jobs, as opposed to manufacturing and industrial jobs, is primarily responsible for this promising news, and growth is expected to be solid at least to 1990.

By mid-1987, according to economic forecasters, services should employ about 23.3 million people, an all-time high. In 1985 alone 1.2 million new jobs were added in this employment sector, including 350,000 new positions in the business services industry and 220,000 in health services, the largest single U.S. industry. Within corporations, the greatest growth will be in clerical, professional and technical jobs.

The composition of tomorrow's information-economy work force is predicted to change in at least three major ways:

- By 1990 there will be fewer younger and older workers, and a significant bulge in the middle-age grouping will appear in comparison with current percentages.
- More women and minorities will continue to pour into the work force, with many moving into technical, professional, and managerial roles.
- Entry-level workers will be better educated, and more will have had special vocational and technical training.

Each of these projections has an important influence on the way Americans will look upon work in the decade to come. While some consequences of these demographic changes seem obvious and inescapable, there will be more than a few surprises since economics and demographics cannot accurately foretell the long-term ramifications of workers' changing *attitudes*.

Younger workers' expectations and aspirations are particularly revealing. A 1984 survey of the attitudes of high-school students aged seventeen and eighteen accurately presaged the current change in attitude toward the prevailing work ethic. Now aged nineteen and twenty and either in college or in entry-level jobs in the workplace, these students provided evidence that the fulfillment-through-work philosophy is far from dead, since 76 percent felt that work would be a central part of their lives. However, it is rapidly being undermined by young workers' expressed interest in other aspects of life. The criteria on which they are basing their career choices are already far different than those of their 1970s counterparts.

For example, 50.3 percent of the high-school students surveyed thought a job that provided a chance to earn a good deal of money was very important, but 41 percent felt that a job that leaves a lot of time for other things in life was equally important. Further, while a job offering high status and prestige was viewed as important by 24.4 percent of those surveyed, more than 71 percent opted for careers in which they could do the things they did best—and more than 89 percent sought work that was "interesting to do." Perhaps most heartening is the fact that half of the young respondents planned to prepare for careers that gave them an opportunity to be directly helpful to others.

- The post–Baby Boom drop in the birth rate, combined with steady growth in service industries, is already resulting in a labor shortage that will allow workers to "pick and choose," demanding more from their jobs than a fancy title and a steady paycheck.

While the Baby Boomers themselves are experiencing some corporate career difficulties as a result of their numbers (though not quite as many as anticipated a few years back), things will be very different for the fewer children they are having through the end of the 1900s. The vastly lower birth rate and the expanding economy of the past twenty years have created an important new trend: increasingly severe labor shortages that will result in a tight labor market through 1999. As reported by John Naisbitt and Patricia Aburdene in *Re-inventing the Corporation,* "Today the two essential elements for corporate transformation are present in our society: new values and economic necessity." To survive, labor-hungry corporations will be forced to recast their personnel policies in acknowledgment of the waning of the "work is everything" ethic. The new corporate environment, prompted by the coming labor shortage, will accommodate a new breed of employee who demands something more from his or her job than a prestigious title and a competitive salary. Much of that something more will be job satisfaction. If the worker's view of the job has changed from something to be hoped for to something to be expected as one's right, then the psychology of entitlement will extend to job satisfaction as well.

A host of research findings on file at the Work In America Institute in Scarsdale, New York, indicate how central job satisfaction is to material, social, and physical well-being. Among the major predictors of life satisfaction in national surveys, for example, are income, occupation, education level, and *job satisfaction*—all of which are inextricably linked with life at work. From both a societal and an organizational perspective, job dissatisfaction will become ever more costly. As Daniel Moynihan has said, "If the quality of life becomes a central concern in our society's third century, then the quality of work life shall as well."

Confronted with an impending labor shortage, companies will need to offer their employees more than steady work. Of equal importance in their recruitment strategies will be opportunities for personal growth, additional control over the structure and content of employees' jobs, and far more flexible schedules. More attractive benefit plans will also become the norm. To attract a competitive share of the most talented workers, which they will need to survive in an increasingly volatile business environment, companies will, in short, have to become better places to work. Where all the moral arguments of the past decade in favor of more humane, employee-oriented policies have fallen on deaf employer ears, the new economic exigencies will spur these desirable changes.

- Because creativity will be the most-sought trait in the worker of tomorrow, organizations will go to surprising lengths to accommodate the needs and even preferences of this new breed of worker.

While it is already widely acknowledged that creativity is the key to future corporate success, U.S. businesses have, until now, done precious little to encourage creative thinking. "In the United States, we've literally beaten out of workers the ability to be creative," says Sharon Kirkman Donegan, president of Boyle/Kirkman Associates, a management consulting firm in Yarmouth Port, Massachusetts. "We try to mold them into very lovely puppets or people who do nothing but repeat what we want them to repeat." In support of her observation, Donegan notes that most of her client companies reward their employees for "everything but creativity."

Increased flexibility, particularly in work schedules, will be one way in which employers reward creative thinkers in future years. As the new critical resource, creativity will be increasingly valued, even when the price tag is employer accommodation to work schedules based almost solely on employees' personal preferences. Since creative people tend to define work in terms of tasks instead of time blocks, they often become so involved in a task that time is forgotten, say psychologists. An example is the graphic artist or architect who becomes so engrossed in a design project that he finds himself still hunched over the drafting board at 3 A.M. But if the design solves a corporate problem and is delivered on schedule, what does it matter if it is accomplished in the wee hours of the morning or that the designer sleeps through the board meeting at which it is eventually presented?

In the years ahead, corporations will be far likelier to accommodate the maverick tendencies of creative personnel in order to access their valuable talents. Further, *creative personnel* will be redefined to include many of those formerly designated as *technical employees:* mechanical engineers and space planners, computer programmers and software developers, insurance investigators and police detectives, problem solvers and trouble shooters—anyone, in short, whose creative energies are best focused on a personal, rather than an organizational, schedule.

The corporations that are successful in recruiting creative employees will recognize their self-management capabilities as well, and will increasingly base salaries on overall performance rather than, say, attendance. As such companies reap the economic rewards of the increased employee commitment and productivity resulting from more flexible personnel policies, the rigid hierarchies of the past will yield to new internal structures characterized by clusters of self-managing "intrapreneurs"—people with entrepreneurial interests and abilities working within large organizations.

Naturally, older workers will experience some misgivings about this new order of things. A Work In America publication, entitled *Straight Line Projections into the Future,* explores the generation gap in the attitudes of those maturing in the 1950s and those maturing in the 1970s toward institutional authority—a gap which may widen appreciably as more younger workers move into positions of greater power and authority within organizations.

> [A] key question is whether older workers and managers . . . will accept these "new breed" employees. Already threatened by technical obsolescence and concerned with the loss of authority traditionally due those in managerial roles, they may lament, "Why can't we get people like we used to?" This may be evident in efforts to discredit the contributions of younger workers, to stifle workplace innovations, and to send the message to subordinates "not to rock the boat."

One way to address this problem, the report suggests, is

to provide for more contact between younger and older workers.

> Research studies have shown that once people get to know one another personally, they tend to discard stereotypes and deal with others on a person-to-person basis. This could go a long way toward clearing up misperceptions each group has of "them." Another is to provide forums in which the realities of this generation gap can be openly discussed and examined with an eye toward mutual accommodation. This is contrary to the present norms of many organizations where conflicts are addressed behind closed doors, but organizations that support a climate of open debate and mutual influence will be seen as the most attractive and innovative in the future.

Because the predicted labor shortage is already emerging at the entry level, corporations are finding it necessary to alter more than work schedules to attract the new breed of worker and retain them, since entrepreneurial opportunities are increasingly appealing to the motivated, creative self-starter. As a result, corporate efforts are redoubling to increase the challenge and variety in specific work assignments, particularly in entry-level jobs, and to enrich them with decision-making aspects. Further, even first-tier workers are allowed more autonomy and freedom from close supervision. Finally, new recruits are receiving a great deal more career counseling early on, plus future-oriented training. In these ways, beginning employees can more clearly see the possibilities for growth within the organization and are less likely to leave it precipitously.

- Baby Boomers, faced with career bottlenecks because of their numbers, will refuse to accept stalled careers, moving out to other organizations or entrepreneurial endeavors when they can no longer move up.

A tremendous amount of flux will occur in the American workplace in the next fifteen years due to the aging of the Baby Boomers. The unprecedented number of middle-aged workers projected as the Boomers reach age forty and beyond has long been anticipated to create a management population explosion within corporations. The consequences predicted have included lower promotion ratios, higher turnover, and more mid-career crises—and to some extent, these have occurred.

Management expert Peter Drucker proclaimed in September 1985 that "Most of the Baby Boomers have gone as far as they will go in management and will stay in their present jobs another thirty years or so."

Joining the gloom-and-doomers, a recent book review in *The New York Times* predicted, "Today there are so many young managers aiming for the same spots at the top that, with the older Baby Boomers closing in on forty, this generation is about to hit the wall."

Despite these discouraging prognostications, the news is not all bad. Much of it, in fact, is extraordinarily good, largely due to the take-charge attitude of the Boomers themselves.

When one speaks with workers of the generation under discussion, the pessimism one expects to confront seems almost nonexistent, reports Myron Magnet in a *Fortune* cover story.

> These young executives . . . believe that the quality of young managers is higher, and the competition sharper, than a generation ago. But even so, they think, the opportunity to rise is as wide open as ever. Proponents of the view that demography is destiny argue that there won't be enough high-level executive slots for the horde of Baby Boom managers who want them, just as

> there wasn't enough space in maternity wards and schools for the 76 million Americans born between 1946 and 1964. But the evidence they marshal usually consists of demographic generalizations, like the observation that the total number of workers aged twenty-five to thirty-four grew 68 percent from 1970 to 1980, reaching nearly 27 million, and the number of managers of the same age grew 110 percent to 1.2 million.

Such figures, taken from reports of the U.S. Census Bureau, are technically accurate but don't tell the real story, Magnet points out. Of all those managers in the statistics, only about half are employed by big business. The rest are involved in the management of fast-food franchises, retail outlets, and new businesses of their own, where the prospects for growth remain excellent. Lumped into the "management" category in Census reports, these noncorporate managers are hard to find on paper, but easy to spot in the real world, where energy and optimism are enabling them to carve out careers for themselves in which the sky's the limit.

In addition, anticipating the mid-career difficulties of their employees, corporations have made it a top priority to unblock the career paths of their managers. Some have developed a second promotional ladder for technical personnel, for example. Another approach is the creation of desirable lateral transfers within the organization. Still another is experimentation with educational sabbaticals, job-sharing, and other, more flexible, career path options. Far-sighted corporations are also placing more and more emphasis on employee career counseling, often retraining workers for second careers within the organization.

In companies that have experienced a promotions bottleneck, the cause is as apt to be economic as demographic, personnel executives point out. Ford Motor

Company is a good example. Over the past ten years, inflation-adjusted salaries of middle managers have declined slightly, Ford reports. However, Ford's growth has slowed significantly over the same period, creating the need for staff reductions instead of the expansions once planned during those years.

But within corporate circles supply and demand continue to fluctuate, and for every Ford-type case history, there is a contrasting situation to report. While some companies may indeed need fewer managers than they have available to them, many others are actively seeking *more*. Here are three such companies, profiled in *Fortune* in early 1986:

- In the past ten years, Allied Corporation increased the number of profit centers from twelve to over fifty. Each has required new management staff.
- American Can Company currently has three times as many jobs with profit-and-loss responsibility as it had in 1970.
- During the early 1950s, Maytag Company experienced enormous growth, forcing the company to hire many new managers who ran the company for the ensuing thirty years. Now this entire tier is moving into retirement, creating a tremendous opportunity for the thirty-five- to forty-two-year-olds waiting in the wings.

The point of all this is that while it is true that demographics are changing significantly in the work force they are not doing so in a static environment. Other things are changing, too—notably, the astounding growth in service-industry job opportunities as a result of our new information-based economy. And typically for this generation, the Baby Boomers are aware that the times, they are a-changing—and are refusing to accept the limitations imposed on them by forecasts based on outdated statistics.

"Though in 1986 the first Baby Boomers are turning forty," reports Myron Magnet,

> their talk still shows a generous measure of youthful bravado. But it registers, beyond the bravado, important changes in attitude from the previous generation. Baby Boom managers truly are unwilling to accept the world as it is handed to them. They are slow to define themselves in terms of their relation to a particular employer or institution. They take change for granted and without timidity precipitate it themselves. Rather than being blocked by the old order, they are ushering in the new. If, as is often said, American industry is trying to revitalize itself, here is the vitality.

Certainly, it is true that the Baby Boomers are reasserting control over their professional fates. Feeling blocked within a given organization, they are increasingly exercising their options to move out into entrepreneurial endeavors or into other organizations, wherever opportunity presents itself. Typical is Marjorie Elsner, age thirty-seven. Joining the personnel administration unit of a Hartford-based insurance company after obtaining a graduate degree in counseling from UCLA, Elsner found herself dispirited by the lack of advancement opportunities available to her as well as by the inflexible policies it fell to her to enforce. "I kept hoping things would get better, for me personally and for insurance employees generally, but I finally had to admit they probably wouldn't."

Though her colleagues advised patience, Elsner opted to change jobs, moving to the human resources development department in the home office of a fast-food franchiser.

> When I was hired, I was told that the company was eager to recruit trainees with good management potential and to revamp their personnel policies to attract more talented women. But after two years of knocking my head against a brick wall, I realized they were merely paying lip service to that philosophy. When it came down to actually changing the *status quo*, management always found some reason not to do it.

Shortly thereafter Elsner moved yet again, this time into partnership with two young men who were launching a small chain of video rental outlets in the Northeast. After three years, she feels she has found a home. "Business is booming," she reports with satisfaction,

> and we probably have the lowest employee turnover rate in the service industry. Finally, I'm in a place where my ideas and proposals really make a difference to the health of the organization and of the workers we employ. We've instituted policies here that would have the old boys at my first two places of employment gagging on their coffee. And they're working!

Even when they are happy with their work in a given company, most Baby Boomers are striving to maintain greater emotional distance from their employers in order to remain autonomous and therefore more readily able to respond to changing opportunities in the future. "I've never felt that I work for this company or that company. I've always considered myself a professional person who works in my own best interests, first and foremost, and in the best interests of whatever company is paying me for as long as it's paying me," says Janet Rosemont, a marketing manager.

> It's just not a good idea to count on a single organization to take care of your future. By keep-

ing control of my own future, I truly feel I'm a more desirable employee for any corporation. I'll never be a hanger-on—deadwood they have to pension off to get rid of me. When it's time to go, I'll be the first to know it, and I'll have something more appropriate to my needs at that time already lined up.

- More women will continue to enter the work force, but they will be far more selective about the jobs they accept, basing their decisions on the need to balance professional and domestic responsibilities.

Changing family structures and simple economic realities will continue to prompt increasing numbers of women to enter or reenter the labor force through 1990, and the decline in the birth rate and the increase in the number of female heads-of-household suggest that they will stay at work for many decades to come. The steadily increasing enrollments of women in universities, and technical and vocational schools also indicates that they are spending longer periods of time preparing for their careers.

Recent surveys indicate that women's job expectations and aspirations will parallel, to a great extent, the changing expectations of men. Jobs will be sought not only to meet economic and self-esteem needs but, increasingly, as a means to contribute in some positive way to America's economy and society.

To attract motivated female workers, corporations will continue the trend of making jobs traditionally viewed as "male" open to women, of evening out pay rates for male and female workers in similar job categories, and increasing the amount of variety and challenge offered by specific jobs.

More than this, at long last measures will be taken to respond to women workers' special needs. These include the provision of more flexible work schedules, job-sharing and part-time work opportunities that leave time for child rearing, new policies that enable women to respond quickly to domestic emergencies such as the illness of a child, and stepped-up referral services for day care and other household services. A greater number of corporations will establish day-care centers on their premises, and maternity leaves and benefits will become institutionalized—if not nationalized, as in other countries.

These long-overdue changes will not, of course, be based on corporate altruism, as was hoped in earlier decades, but upon economic necessity born of the growing labor shortage. The fact is, if employing organizations expect to recruit and retain talented female workers, they will no longer have a choice.

For their part, women will become increasingly selective about their choice of employers, "hiring" those whose policies are most closely attuned not only to their professional priorities but to their ongoing need to fulfill multiple roles on and off the job.

- Older workers will have the best of all worlds—the chance to retire early on generous pensions, if that is their choice, or new opportunities for second (or third or fourth) careers.

Of all the demographic segments of the work force, older workers have perhaps the brightest prospects in the years ahead. For one thing, the potential end of mandatory retirement laws and the growing trend toward second and third careers suggest that the specter of enforced retirement may be banished for those who choose to continue working in their later years. Today, there is much evidence that stereotypes regarding the learning abilities, memories, energy levels, and orientations toward risk and innovation of older workers are crumbling. The "old fogies" have become the "gray panthers"— a societal force to be reckoned with.

"We are finally shaking the model that had us joining a corporation at age twenty-two, becoming vice president at age forty-five and maybe president at fifty-five," says Alex, a professor of business education at a private New England university.

> If you didn't achieve the presidency, you turned into an embittered old fossil that they pensioned off at age sixty-five. That was a "normal" career model up until quite recently, and it was based on the assumption that you're vigorous in your twenties and thirties, starting to decline in your forties, a deteriorating specimen in your fifties, and ready for a wheelchair in your sixties.
>
> In fact, though, we're staying vigorous much longer, and people who are active decade after decade aren't going to stay in one company and continue to describe the curve of rising and declining powers that was assumed to be the norm in the past. Quitting and starting over—or retiring from one job and beginning another—is increasingly the norm today.

Eric Knudson, an organizational management consultant and entrepreneur who is himself a veteran of the corporate trenches, concurs.

> There is a lot going on in today's economy that will accelerate the need for career changes in later years, and anyone who plans to work for an extended length of time must be aware of this. Older workers, in particular, must face the need to plan carefully for second careers as they approach the traditional retirement age. There are hundreds of thousands of people in this country who are physically and mentally active well into their eighties who simply do not wish to retire.

Knudson does not believe, as some do, that eliminating mandatory retirement policies is a realistic expectation, however.

> Though there is a movement afoot to eliminate or modify mandatory retirement policies, I don't think they will change significantly—nor do I think they really should. Many people in the sixty to sixty-five age group are, after all, no longer as competent as they once were because of failing physical health, mental agility, burnout, technical obsolescence, and a variety of other factors. They represent a hefty percentage of the senior work force, and many either do not recognize their impairments or refuse to do anything about them. Further, the employees in this category are generally earning peak salaries due to longevity, adding insult to injury from an employer's perspective. Thus, an employer must have some mechanism to move such workers into more suitable situations through retirement or retraining.

The growing need to reduce the heavy economic burden imposed on organizations by senior employees is typified, Knudson says, by the actions of three major insurance companies during the first half of 1982, reported in the *Wall Street Journal:*

- Continental Corporation offered 1400 of its employees over the age of fifty-five early retirement with a lump sum six-month salary payment and supplemental payments to make up for Social Security benefits lost by those retiring before their sixty-second birthdays.
- Prudential Insurance offered 1700 of its older employees as much as a year's salary to take

early retirement in order to "open the pipeline" for promotions for minorities and women.

- Metropolitan Life Insurance Company offered 500 employees in its New York and San Francisco offices, most of whom were in their fifties, up to a year and a half's salary to take early retirement.

These and hundreds of other companies who have since made similar offers to their senior employees are doing so out of economic necessity, but the negative connotation of the "golden handshake" in years past has been replaced. Far from being something to be dreaded, early retirement has become the favorite fantasy of middle-age workers. Because most early retirement packages are so attractive, they now represent an exciting and well-deserved opportunity for the older worker to have the best of both worlds. In the course of his or her total work years, today's worker can anticipate having the salary, position, and prestige offered by traditional corporate employment, followed by a decade or two more of more personally pleasing, nontraditional employment working for oneself or as a part-time worker in a job geared specifically to the older worker, all with the secure financial base provided by early retirement benefits.

- Workers of all kinds—those just starting out, blocked Baby Boomers, women seeking more flexibility, and older workers starting on second careers—will find more entrepreneurial opportunities than ever before awaiting them.

There have always been people who chafed within the confines of the corporate structure—rugged individualists who opted for the risky but exciting life of the entrepreneur. In the years ahead, however, more workers than ever before will take the road less traveled, branching out on their own to find professional and personal fulfillment.

"Go for it, America," urged President Reagan in a 1985 address regarding his proposal for restructuring the current income-tax schedule. Though opinions on his tax proposal varied widely, no one could help but applaud the president's efforts to rekindle the flame of entrepreneurial endeavor in this country.

Is there a worker who has not, at one time or another, longed to go into business for himself or herself? An ambitious employee who doesn't believe in his heart of hearts that he could run the company better than the boss, given half a chance? The enormous popularity of such 1980s movies as *9 to 5* and *Take This Job and Shove It* render these questions rhetorical. It is entrepreneurism, to a large extent, that symbolizes the American Dream. In this country, as in perhaps no other, a person with a good idea and a commitment to making it work can still make fantasy into reality.

But working for oneself is only part of the fantasy. For thousands of frustrated commuters, weary of the transportation, financial, domestic, political, and myriad other hassles associated with traditional nine-to-five employment outside the home, entrepreneurism offers the opportunity to control the kind of work one does, when one does it, and most importantly, *where* one does it. And with every passing day, a greater number of Americans are choosing to work at home.

"Home-based businesses are one of the fastest-growing sectors of the American economy," reports Samuel A. Schreiner, Jr., in the January 1986 issue of *Reader's Digest*.

> Estimates are that as many as 10 million people are currently making a living at home. People increasingly want to work at what they like and to have control of their own time and income. At

the same time, while the country has moved toward an economy based on information processing and personal services, profitable new opportunities have been created. According to an AT&T survey, 41 percent of residential households that are home to a business have incomes of $30,000 or more. It's not surprising, then, that a recent Yankelovich, Skelly and White poll showed that earning a living at home is the secret dream of fully a third of American workers.

Here are some of the latest statistics on this phenomenon:

- Over the past fifteen years, the number of self-employed Americans has nearly doubled, growing from 5.7 million to nearly 11 million. (Excluding agricultural workers, the number is 7.5 million.)
- New businesses are springing up at the rate of 700,000 every year—eight times more than in the 1950s.

Other indicators abound. In 1985, for example, Time, Inc., created a new publication called *Home Office*, aimed specifically at businesspersons who work at home. In doing so, Time joined the publishers of *Entrepreneur*, *In Business*, and *Mother Earth News* in the self-employed readers' market.

A brief perusal of our local library's card catalog turned up more than twenty recently published books on the subject of self-employment, from *The Best of Both Worlds: A Guide to Home-Based Careers* by Joan Wester Anderson to *Worksteads: Living and Working in the Same Place* by J. J. Hewes.

At least five newsletters exist to offer moral and financial support to the home-based worker, many of which are published by flourishing associations—the

National Alliance of Homebased Businesswomen and the National Association for the Cottage Industry, to name only two.

An entire service industry has sprung up to accommodate the needs of the professional, home-based worker, providing temporary office space and conference facilities, administrative services, telecommunications, mail and call forwarding, and a host of related services. Notable is The Headquarters Companies, which provides such amenities in sixty-six locations throughout the country—eighteen sites in California alone!

With all this support available, going into business for oneself is no longer considered the act of a maverick, and in our new information-based economy, money (capital) is no longer the most critical resource for entrepreneurial success. Personal knowledge, ability, and creativity are the key elements required, and the person who discovers an unmet need and devises a profitable way to meet it needs only a desk and a telephone to start a business successfully.

The products and services offered by self-employed entrepreneurs range from clerical and catering to technical research and product development. Many home-based businesspersons are finding it especially lucrative to cater to the needs of those who choose to work *outside* the home—a happy symbiosis for all concerned. Women are especially alert to such opportunities, and their intense need for flexibility, rooted in the domestic double standard* that still dictates that women be primarily responsible for child rearing and homemaking, has created a tidal wave of female entrepreneurs.

Unable to find satisfying jobs within organizations that meet their needs to be available in the event of domestic emergencies, to nurture their children with

---

*See *Working It Out: The Domestic Double Standard* by Judith K. Sprankle, Walker and Co., New York, New York, 1986.

varying intensity over the years, and to keep all their professional and personal interests on the front burner simultaneously, women now own something like 30 percent of all American businesses. Though this may be a surprising statistic, it is *not* surprising that a large number of these businesses deal in products and services designed for women. Day-care centers are a notable example, and with a 50,000-center demand contrasted with the current 9,000-center supply, the opportunities in the field remain legion.

The decision to become an entrepreneur is generally prompted by personal needs, as well as by workers' failure to accommodate their preferences on someone else's payroll. These include a desire to be paid fairly in direct proportion to effort, a need for independence rooted in an intense dislike of deferring to an employer's wishes, the excitement and challenge of being in charge, and a strong need to achieve. Working for oneself has become the job of choice for millions of Americans who have put together the precise elements of schedule, compensation, challenge, self-esteem, creativity, and whatever else adds up to exactly the right combination for *them*.

- Overall, American workers will forego the workaholic tendencies of the past two decades, opting for more balanced lives in which work has a prominent place but is not the single most dominant factor.

While the restructuring of corporate policies and the expansion of entrepreneurial possibilities will do much to create the *opportunity* for more balanced, personally fulfilling lives, the most significant future trend will be American workers' determination to take advantage of that opportunity in the years ahead.

Workaholism is most often, after all, a self-imposed way of life. The true workaholic is generally enamored of the idea of work itself, loves work, and resents being dragged away from it. Increasingly, though, even dedicated workaholics are acknowledging the severe limitations of their way of life and are consciously choosing to change their ways. In future years, most people who work eighteen hours a day will do so only because financial burdens make such a schedule temporarily necessary. Obviously, financial emergencies will continue to arise and be dealt with via moonlighting and other forms of involuntary overwork.

For the most part, though, the era in which the employer calls every shot, demanding extraordinary levels of round-the-clock enthusiasm and effort seven days a week in accordance with the work ethic of recent decades, is over. No longer will workers allow themselves to be victimized by true workaholic bosses—or by unreasonably demanding clients who expect them to be on call day and night.

The relative financial security afforded by the two-earner potential in most modern families will permit nearly every worker to select work that is personally, even if not particularly financially, rewarding; to change jobs as many as five times over the course of a career; to combine paid employment with emotionally satisfying volunteer work or child rearing; to intersperse periods of paid employment with planned periods of unemployment to pursue advanced educational or other goals; to risk the hazards of self-employment; and increasingly, to retire from the work force when it is the employee's, rather than the employer's idea.

The bottom line is that the work force of the future will represent a broader cross section of society than ever before, and each subgroup will bring to the work place its special concerns and interests. Economic security will continue to be the basic motivation for paid employment, but, simultaneously, growing numbers of well-educated males and females, whites and minorities, will view interesting work and the chance to use their talents fully, as well as to grow personally and professionally, as their just due.

As jobs become easier to come by in the imminent era of labor shortages, workers will increasingly turn their attention to the quality of life as a whole, not merely the quality of their work lives. The work ethic of the past two decades will thus be supplanted by an ethic that puts work in its place—and keeps it there.

INDEX